NEW AGE COMES TO MAIN STREET

What Worried Christians Must Know

Lowell D. Streiker

Abingdon Press/Nashville

NEW AGE COMES TO MAIN STREET

Copyright © 1990 by Abingdon Press

This book is printed on acid-free paper.

Library of Congress Cataloging-in-Publication Data

Streiker, Lowell D.
    New Age comes to Main Street : what worried Christians must know / Lowell D. Streiker.
      p. cm.
    Includes bibliographical references.
    ISBN 0-687-27715-9 (alk. paper)
    1. New Age movement—Controversial literature. 2. Occultism-Religious aspects—Christianity—Controversial literature.
    3. Cults—United States—Controversial literature.
    4. Parapsychology—Religious aspects—Christianity—Controversial literature. I. Title.
BP605.N48   1990
299'.93—dc20   89-27340
                                     CIP

MANUFACTURED IN THE UNITED STATES OF AMERICA

To
Cuddles and Gus,
my constant companions

CONTENTS

INTRODUCTION

A man's work is nothing but this slow trek to redis-
cover, through the detours of art, those two or three
great and simple images in whose presence his heart
first opened.

—Albert Camus,
preface to *The Wrong Side and the Right Side*

Throughout my life, there have been two or three images
in whose presence my heart has opened. I have found them
again and again, sometimes in "the detours of art," but more
often in the world of religious experience. The images, as
Camus suggests, are at once simple and profound. In a single
moment of awareness, they combine symbols, pictures, and
feelings, a movement away from what has been toward what
is intuitively grasped as possible. These moments expose us to
the raw power within ourselves, our world, and being itself.
Such moments drag us (sometimes willingly, sometimes
kicking and screaming) into a spiritual existence, a dangerous
journey fraught with the perils of ambiguity and the pitfalls
of ambivalence. They invite us to an intimate, loving relationship with the mysterious other that is always present and
for which we seem to have no choice but to search with all the
strength we can muster. Moreover, they offer us an effortless
return, a resting on a reality that is neither found by searching nor embraced by loving.

9

This book is an essay on religious experience. It relates how powerful intuitions, unforgettable states of awareness, and unusual occurrences of an individual's existence are interpreted, confirmed, and made the basis of a way of life. The point of these accounts is that wonderful, confusing, even bizarre things happen, and that what they mean depends on many, many factors.

In particular, this book is an inquiry into the meaning and significance of a contemporary family of cultural and religious experiences popularly known as "New Age." In the following pages, we shall meet New Age personages, forms of expression, and life-styles. There are, as we shall see, two kinds of New Age phenomena. There is "left hand" or "ecstatic" New Age, the New Age of gurus, channelers (also known as "channels," "transchannels," or "mediums"), psychics, Witches, crystal healers, and other visionaries. And there is "right hand" or "social transformationist" New Age, the realm of ecology, social conscience, feminism, responsible investing, and compassion for all creatures.

My focus is on local manifestations of New Age. I am much more fascinated by the way that New Age has come to main street than the way it is presented by *People* magazine, "ABC Evening News," the *New York Times,* or the latest supernatural horror movie. I have deliberately sought out harbingers of the Age of Aquarius in my community, neighboring communities, and diverse local communities throughout the United States. The forms of New Age that interest me are those accessible to ordinary folk, whether or not they have sat at the feet of the media-heralded stars of New Age or read all of the Aquarian best sellers. New Age is not limited to, nor particularly well represented by, Shirley MacLaine, Kevin Ryerson, and Marilyn Ferguson. Nor is it adequately understood or interpreted by its critics.

Even as I write this book, the term *New Age* is losing its usefulness. The social transformationists have all but surrendered the expression to the ecstatics; among themselves, the media and the ecstatics have virtually reduced New Age to the status of a fad. Meanwhile, New Age continues to insinuate itself into places of the heart and imagination, guaranteeing that neither form of New Age is in any danger of fading away when media attention finds someplace new to play. As I shall argue throughout these pages, New Age is not new. It is more than a fad, and it shows every sign of enduring. In the midst of the hype, quackery, foolishness, and foolhardiness, there are permanent, vital, and abiding elements. If the labels "New Age" and "Aquarian" become worn, discard them. Nothing will be lost.

Tides, Eddies, and Backwaters

What is the current status of New Age? A parallel to the Civil War winter of 1862–1863 comes to mind. Bruce Catton says of those months:

> Profound currents were moving in America . . . but they had not yet fused to form one great tide that would carry everything along with it. They were still separate, often in conflict, with deep swirling eddies to mark the points of tension, and with odd backwaters where things seemed to drift upstream; and no one could say how the business would finally be resolved.[1]

This volume presents the "deep swirling eddies," "the points of tension," and the "odd backwaters." How the business will finally be resolved, I cannot say. But I have some ideas on the subject.

Finally, I have attempted to draw some spiritual, ethical, and social lessons from New Age. In so doing, I am operating as a kind of religion critic. I have examined and reviewed New Age much as theater critics, literary critics, or motion picture critics examine their respective art forms. I have tried to distinguish between good religion and bad religion, between useful forms of expression and useless forms of expression, between what is valuable and what is worthless. In the process, I have gone beyond criticism and offered my own articulations of some basic New Age insights.

In some cases, I have suggested that certain New Age formulas should be reinterpreted or abandoned. By so doing, I have hoped to stir up discussions of various sorts on the part of various discussants. Let me explain. First, I want to stimulate New Agers to be more careful and responsible in articulating what they believe as well as the rules by which they live (and expect others to live). Second, I would like to see Christians of various camps take New Age seriously. New Age is not a joke, not a satanic conspiracy, not an infection, not mad ravings that will go away if we just ignore them. Third, I hope that on the basis of the distinctions drawn and the formulations attempted, the New Ager may begin talking to the Christian and the Christian to the New Ager. It may turn out that each has a great deal to teach the other and to learn from the other as well. There are so few moments for any human being in which the heart is opened to the mystery of being. It is a shame when the full impact of such moments is lost because the telling of them catches in our throats due to our reticence or is excluded from our hearing by our prejudices.

The best summary of what I have essayed here was suggested to me by a chance remark I happened to overhear one day: "Each age is a day that is dying for one that is coming to birth." The seriousness of the speaker's tone suggested to me that he was saying something more profound than "Today is the first day of the rest of your life" or some other equally callow bumper-sticker nostrum. I loved the ambiguity of "dying for." Proponents of New Age thinking have been telling the rest of us for some time that one age is over, is moribund, is dying, is dead without knowing it, and that a new way of living and responding—one for which we are desperately waiting—has broken out in our midst like an epidemic of measles. (My established traditionalist acquaintances, of course, protest that the news of the demise of old ways has been greatly exaggerated.)

Will this New Age—whatever it may be—drive a stake through the heart of outmoded assumptions, attitudes, and values? Is it a fad and a fraud? Is it an endless striving after something delicious and desirable that is just beyond our reach? Will it save us and our world? And if so, from what and for what? Or, to sum up all our questions, have the profound currents finally come together to form an irresistible tide?

Flying

In my childhood years, I could not tell the difference between dreams and waking reality. The memories of things that happened in dreams were every bit as clear and convincing as memories of things that happened while I was awake. I would argue with my parents about places we had visited together, restaurants where we had eaten, theaters where we had seen movies, stores where we had shopped, friends whose homes we had visited, gadgets we had tinkered with. How could they have forgotten?

Soon my own experience told me that I was living in two incompatible universes. Underground passageways that I had discovered in the basement of a building one day were gone the next. Toys with which I had been entertained yesterday no longer existed today. And my powers and abilities were becoming so unreliable. I could fly—I had been able to for years—not the way Superman or Captain Marvel flew, many stories high with arms stretched straight ahead. I was able to glide just above the surface of the ground, standing erect like an ice skater. Long strides would carry me three or four feet before I gently touched down. Staircases were my forte. I remembered clearly gliding from the top to the bottom of a long, brass railed, marble stairway beneath the Marbro theater. I never touched a single step.

I needed to test my power. In a sense, that is what my whole life has been about.

CHAPTER ONE

What Is "New Age"?

In 1988 most ultra-conservatives would say that the enemy is the paganism of the New Age, not the secularism of public humanists. Times change.
—Martin E. Marty, *Context*

Now panentheism is not pantheism. Pantheism, which . . . robs God of transcendence, states that "everything is God and God is everything." Panentheism, on the other hand . . . slips in the little Greek word *en* and thus means, "God is in everything and everything is in God. . . ." It is not theistic because it does not relate to God as subject or object, but neither is it pantheistic. Panentheism is a way of seeing the world sacramentally . . . the primary sacrament is creation itself—which includes every person and being who lives.
—Matthew Fox, *Original Blessing: A Primer on Creation Spirituality*

What exactly is New Age? Is it one of those untidy "cultural movements" that seem to hover over us like some invisible cloud of gas—something tangible in its effects, but impossible to observe or define? It has come to main street, it impinges on our consciousness like the fragrance of expensive perfume worn by a beautiful stranger on an elevator or like the odor of a cheap cigar. There is something in the air. But what is it?

One way to discover just what New Age is is to explore how it is defined by proponents, critics, and other observers. As we shall see, many of the distinctive hallmarks of Aquarian religion, attitudes, and ways of living are derived from such historic movements as New Thought, Spiritualism, Theosophy, and Vedantic Hinduism. While New Age may be said to be a stream of spirituality older than America, the fact remains that many elements of New Age manifestations of the past twenty years are unique to this period. For example, personal computers have provided new ways to share information and to participate openly or anonymously in both local and national movements.

BBS Replies

Since, as a computer hobbyist, I spend much of my spare time networking via remote bulletin board systems, I thought I would leave a general query on several systems—including one for my fellow United Church of Christ ministers—and on various "New Age boards." I asked for definitions of New Age, but I received very few. On one New Age system, I received a message from someone who uses as his handle the name of a Native American. We shall call him "Brown Elk." He said:

New Age. . . .
That can be a very difficult concept for some, as it means different things to different people. New Age to me is power. Plain and simple. The ability to control your innermost power and the power you might reflect is the meaning to me.

A minister of a major denomination responded:

> Ah! Humble personal opinion of venerable old fence-sitter
> is besought! I think it is crap, pablum, heresy, self-delusion,
> autoerotic nonsense. But I listen to it to learn what the kids are
> talking about; to learn how we have failed them in the church;
> to learn what has turned them off in the way we've done it.
>
> At my most charitable, which overtakes me about once a
> month, I think there may be under the manure a kernel of
> truth, a dim light, a fragment of the Christ-truth obscured but
> shining dimly; just because "at first was the Word, and
> everything (even New Age rhetoric) was made by that
> Word. . . ."
>
> Now . . . refix inscrutable smile on venerable face, ah, just
> so!
>
> *Thanks* for asking. What do *you* have to say about all this
> "New Agey" stuff?

My reply: "Needless to say as the author of proposed book,
I am answering the question by writing about it. I'll let you
know how the answer turns out. Thanks for the reply."

Time, Times, and Graves

I surveyed various articles on New Age in mass circulation
periodicals. One of the more informative pieces, a *Time*
magazine cover story, exclaimed:

> So here we are in the New Age, a combination of spirituality
> and superstition, fad and farce, about which the only thing
> certain is that it is not new. Nobody seems to know exactly
> where the term came from, but it has been around for several
> decades or more, and many elements of the New Age, like
> faith healing, fortune-telling and transmigration of souls, go
> back for centuries.[1]

Russell Chandler, the celebrated religion writer of the *Los
Angeles Times*, explains:

The expression "New Age" swept into vogue in the 1970s and 1980s, helped along by circulation of the *New Age Journal* and a book by Mark Satin called *New Age Politics*. Marilyn Ferguson's best-selling *Aquarian Conspiracy*, a compendium of the New Age social agenda and philosophical vision, attained status as the unofficial scripture of the movement.

But if Ferguson wrote the New Age "Bible," Shirley MacLaine is its high priestess.[2]

Writing in New Age Journal's *1988 Guide to New Age Living*, Florence Graves, former editor and associate publisher, observes: "There's a lot of confusion now surrounding new age, a term that has been used in the mass media to characterize everything from 'healing' crystals to progressive business consultants." She states that in preparing this guide, "we talked to philosophers, writers, publishers, social critics, and scientists who have been involved in new age issues for a number of years." She notes "Like us, they are very disturbed by the fact that the term is being used these days to describe a number of questionable pursuits. Some are so concerned that they have disavowed any connection with the name." She elaborates:

> In the popular lexicon, new age has become a convenient catchall phrase even less descriptive than the words Democrat or Christian. Does Democrat refer to Jesse Jackson or Henry "Scoop" Jackson? Their beliefs are very different. Does Christian connote Jerry Falwell fundamentalism, Billy Graham populism, or Pope John Paul II traditionalism? These too are very different.[3]

For Graves, New Age is "an amorphous cultural tradition." While it has "both political and spiritual dimensions, it is neither a political party nor a religion."

So what then is "New Age"? Perhaps the critics of New Age can help us.

The Scientific Critique

For some writers, New Age is a grab-bag term for a number of pseudoscientific or anti-scientific tendencies. In his book, *New Age: Notes of a Fringe-Watcher,* science essayist Martin Gardiner subjects Shirley MacLaine, channeling, crystal healing, and various psychics to scrutiny and ridicule. Several other books and periodicals take the same approach. They effectively deflate overblown pretensions and remind us of the human limitations of major figures in the spiritual/psychic limelight. But do they tell us anything about what New Age is and where it comes from? For example, Gardiner derides Immanuel Swedenborg for his "absurd" beliefs about life on other planets. Does Swedenborg's failure as a "psychic astronomer" discredit his psychological and theological insights, prove that his visions were bogus, and eradicate the positive contribution he has made to the tens of thousands who find his teachings central to their lives?

The Evangelical Assault

In *New Age Rage,* the staff of the fundamentalist Spiritual Counterfeits Project criticize New Age as an Eastern, pantheistic, relativistic, amoral, and psychologically harmful alternative to evangelical Christianity. They and many other evangelicals regard New Age as a kind of theological/cultural "yellow peril," a Trojan horse from "the East," that has infiltrated and undermined the very foundations of our way of life. Brooks Alexander, one of the founders of Spiritual Counterfeits Project (SCP) and its current executive director, sees New Age as an unstoppable force, subverting not only the Judeo-Christian synthesis that we call American society, but also spreading its tentacles into the churches of the land, corrupting and replacing the gospel of Jesus Christ. Writing in the *SCP Bulletin,* Alexander says:

> The New Age movement is a media phenomenon, and its identity is a media creation. Of course, its components—the psychics, occultists, mystics, gurus, and exploiters that make it up—have been around for decades, if not forever.[4]

He is displeased that New Age, a "new and positive name" has replaced the denigrating term *occult*, with its "sinister overtones" and "unsavory associations." Referring to the success of the TV miniseries "Out on a Limb," Alexander maintains, "No one seemed to notice that deep cultural and spiritual values had been glibly reversed in the process." In other words, New Age, which Alexander does not like, is no longer described in pejorative terms. But at the same time recent attention to American fundamentalism "has deepened the public's perception that biblical Christians are self-righteous, money-grubbing hypocrites and narrow-minded, hate-mongering buffoons." Alexander's avowed purpose is to invert these attitudes, so that the SCP version of Christianity is always described approvingly, while anything else is exposed as hollow and false.

In a June 1988 interview, Alexander notes that the organized cults that were so often in the media a few years ago are on the decline. But the New Age Movement (NAM) represents an anti-Christian onslaught on the churches "with such historical magnitude that we can never get leverage on it." Alexander relates: "The real issue increasingly is New Age thinking and New Age practices influencing the church." He ruminates: "It's very difficult to be optimistic about the future. The world view is changing to the one that prevailed in the decline side of the Roman Empire—to paganism and a pseudo-scientific form of pantheism." Because of the spread of the New Age perspective, declares Alexander's associate, Robert Burrows, "I think the culture is going to be increasingly hostile to the Christian message."[5]

Other evangelicals assault New Age as a worldwide, satanically fomented attempt to gain control of and/or destroy the planet. Witchcraft, the occult, astrology, and all manner of New Age cultural accretions are uncritically mushed in with the Nazis, organized crime, international drug trafficking, and white slavery to form the satanic New Age collusion. The title (but not the content) of *The Aquarian Conspiracy*, Marilyn Ferguson's wrap-up of personal and social transformative organizations, offers aid and comfort to such theories. New Age is hazardous to your faith and sanity says one set of evangelicals. New Age is a snake in the dark, ready to destroy your family, your home, and your world, says the other. The problem is that none of these evangelical critiques are based on direct examination of New Age phenomena. They rely instead on careless readings of popular literature and the self-serving testimonies and the attendant atrocity stories told by ex-New Agers who have become born-again Christians. One looks in vain for careful sociological, historical, or psychological analyses of Aquarian experiences in the evangelical diatribes.

In addition, much of the conservative assault on New Age is based on the assumption that whatever is not of God (in reality, what is not according to a particular sectarian interpretation of Christianity) is of the devil. Whenever a New Age group attempts to defend itself against the accusation that it worships Satan, it is reminded by opponents that whether or not it acknowledges Satan, it belongs to him nonetheless. For example, when Christian apologists are criticized for confusing Witchcraft and devil worship, they are likely to respond: "From my point of view, whatever is not of Christ is of the devil." But according to my faith, whatever is not of God—that is, whatever is not in accordance with my particular interpretation of the divine—is of God, whether I know it or not.

Kilham's Overkill

In Search of the New Age, Chris Kilham's rather gross parody of New Age movements and their gurus, begins as follows:

For the last decade or more, the term "New Age" has been bandied about liberally. . . . But what is the New Age? Is it a period of time? Is it a collection of ideas? Or is it an emerging culture, whose shared values and ideals are spawning a vast array of philosophies, products, services, and activities?

Without ever attempting a definition, Kilham continues:

Whatever the New Age, one thing is certain: this phenomenon has insinuated itself deeply into our culture. It has become part of the warp and woof of our social fabric. We speak of good vibes, organic foods, karma, acupuncture, and spiritual masters as though they had always been part of our language and life-style. Yet such is not the case. The emergence of the New Age represents one of the most rapidly growing trends ever observed in modern history.[6]

If Kilham's description is accurate, New Age is not so new after all. It is merely the return of the countercultural artifacts of the Hippie period of not so long ago. So why has this trend returned, and what accounts for its cultural imperialism? Kilham never informs us.

Fong-Torres and Adult Hippiedom

According to Ben Fong-Torres, staff writer for the *San Francisco Chronicle*, "pursuing a serious definition of the New Age is, in large measure, a trivial pursuit." Manifestations of New Age seem as ubiquitous as the telephone. Fong-Torres declares:

Every step of the way, one encounters channels and spirits and gurus and psychics and holistic healers reading auras, tarot cards, I Ching and Viking runes; checking chakras; balancing yins and yangs and left-brains with right; exorcising demons and leading breathing exercises and visualizations; and talking, endlessly talking about "transformation. . . ."
New Age books have boomed since [Shirley] MacLaine's

miniseries ["Out on a Limb"]. Her own books have sold more than 8 million copies. [Marilyn] Ferguson's "The Aquarian Conspiracy" has sold more than 500,000 copies. Bernie Siegel's book, "Love, Medicine and Miracles," recently topped the New York Times best-sellers list.[7]

Fong-Torres is convinced that "just as computer magazines crowded newsstands a half-dozen years ago, so do New Age titles today." He lists New Age emporia that offer not only books and crystals, but also toys, novelties, books, music, and videotapes. There are New Age restaurants and even New Age rock and roll night spots. He adds: "There's a New Age comedian and there have been New Age plays. There are New Age dentists and New Age health clinics, New Age slacks (Chi Pants) and New Age board games.[8]

The sense of dissatisfaction with the status quo and the yearning for alternatives sound familiar. Are we witnessing the return of the Hippies and the other college-aged countercultural attitudes of a generation ago? No, says Fong-Torres. For the key word today is *adults*. "The New Age," he insists, "is not an '80s version of the '60s youth movement."[9]

After sampling some of the wonders and inanities of the Age of Aquarius around the San Francisco Bay area, he concludes that New Age phenomena cannot be subsumed under a single definition. He explains: "New Age is not a movement at all; it's a number of separate organizations, nonconformists and adventurers challenging conventional notions."[10]

As I shall point out in these pages, some of the nonconformists and adventurers are challenging the conventional notions of religion; others are rejecting conventional mores and moralities; many are attacking our social structure with its exploitation and marginalization of oppressed minorities. Some are merely fed up but offer no alternatives; others collect weirdness and novelty for their own sake; a few offer well integrated life-styles based on insights, hunches, and dreams as well as profound experiences of personal renewal. Many are trapped in clichés and unexamined assumptions. As Fong-Torres remarks: "It is numbing to hear, over and over again, about the interconnectedness of us all, about how we make our own reality, about being joyous and nurturing on this planet; about being whole, empowered and transformative. . . . I mean, chill out, already!"[11]

Tarcher's Perennial Philosophy

Another significant voice attempting to explain what New Age is (and is not) is Jeremy P. Tarcher, president of Jeremy P. Tarcher, Inc., a major publisher of New Age books. One of his firm's greatest successes has been Marilyn Ferguson's *The Aquarian Conspiracy*. Other Tarcher books include *Channeling* by Jon Klimo, *The Meditative Mind* by Daniel Goleman, *The Search for the Beloved* by Jean Houston, *Chop Wood, Carry Water* by Rick Fields et al., *Drawing on the Right Side of the Brain* by Betty Edwards, *Women Who Love Too Much* by Robin Norwood, *Homeopathic Medicine at Home* by Maesimund B. Panos and Jane Heimlich, and *Bodymind* by Ken Dychtwald. For Tarcher, New Age is not a period of time so much as "a metaphor for a process of striving for personal growth through which millions of people are trying to become more fully awake to their inherent capacities." He is convinced that the New Age world view is based on fundamental assumptions about "the place of humanity in the cosmos."[12] These assumptions may be summarized as follows:

1. The world, including the human race, constitutes an expression of a higher, more comprehensive divine nature.
2. Hidden within each human being is a higher

divine self, which is a manifestation of the higher, more comprehensive divine nature.

3. This higher nature can be awakened and can become the center of the individual's everyday life.
4. This awakening is the reason for the existence of each individual life.

These assumptions, says Tarcher in concert with Aldous Huxley, are part of "the Perennial Philosophy," which is "perhaps the oldest underlying spiritual perspective of humanity." Hence, he claims, "the New Age is not new—it is ancient."[13]

Tarcher observes that most New Agers have undergone some kind of personal awakening or transformation that has "changed their views of the world and of their goals in life."[14] When these newly awakened seekers attempt to apply their insights to the world in which they live and work, they are often confused and frustrated. They discover, reports Tarcher, that the task of embodying enlightenment is "invariably larger than the ability of the individual to contain or reflect it." Tarcher explains: "Inevitably, this preliminary self-realization, this connection to new ideas and higher values, is accompanied by a massive shaking up of the individual's traditional perspectives. These are often replaced by more open, experimental, idiosyncratic ideas and behaviors."[15]

Because the media have focused on the fringe activities of the New Age (reincarnation, extraterrestrials, crystals, psychics, channeling, and the amount of money that is expended on New Age products and services), they have ignored the efforts at personal and social transformation arising from the inherent Perennial Philosophy. Tarcher succinctly comments, "The press have reported the carnival side show and not the acts in the big tent."[16]

New Agers, he insists, are not crazy. For the most part, he argues, "they are ordinary people who have shared some

extraordinary experiences, who have awakened to the wider
possibilities of the heart and mind, and who are trying their
best to fit these perceptions into daily life in a culture that is in
general unsympathetic to them."[17] But Tarcher would not
have to insist on the mundaneness and sanity of the New Age
if New Age phenomena did not, at first glance, appear
neither sane nor ordinary. If I understand him correctly, he
is saying that New Age phenomena are essentially spiritual.
More often than not, they are the product of personal
conversion. As such they can be messy, traumatic, and
confused. But beneath the disorder is a vision of the way that
the world and the life of the individual ought to be and a
sense of direction for achieving this vision.

Peters' Principles

A friendly critic of New Age, Ted Peters, professor of
systematic theology at Berkeley's Pacific Lutheran Theological
Seminary, describes the movement as "a phenomenon of
cultural consciousness," consisting of "a set of cosmological ideas
and spiritual practices that are widely shared by diverse groups
and individuals."[18] He enumerates eight of these ideas: (1) the
search for wholism; (2) monism or pantheism; (3) belief in a
transpersonal self that unites us at a mystical level with other
selves; (4) the conviction that each of us has a potential that can be
awakened through various educative techniques; (5) reincarnation; (6) an incipient eschatology that envisions a radical
transformation of human existence and of the world; (7) reliance
on knowledge or consciousness-raising as the means of
salvation/transformation; and (8) accepting Jesus as a teacher
through whose personal example and mystical doctrine we can
achieve our own salvation. Peters chastises New Age for being
naive and unrealistic. He asserts:

> The world we live in is not essentially a whole. It is broken by
> sin and death and is alienated from its divine creator.

> . . . This brokenness is not an illusion that can be corrected
> through consciousness-raising; it is real. The power necessary
> to heal this brokenness and make things whole again does not
> lie within. Rather it comes to us from beyond, from our
> original creative source, God's grace . . . it comes eschatolo-
> gically, in the promised transformation.[19]

While I agree with Peters' theological stance, I find his
description of New Age inaccurate and his criticism
somewhat poorly aimed. His attack relies on buzz words like
monism, pantheism, reincarnation, and *eschatology,* which he does
not define and which mean one thing in his theological
universe and several others among various representatives of
New Age thinking. This semantic carelessness can easily
degenerate into a kind of sophisticated name-calling. For
example, while I have conversed with the adherents of
hundreds of spiritual traditions, sects, and movements, I
have never in my life met a self-proclaimed monist (one who
believes that only God exists) or a pantheist (one who believes
that everything is God and God is everything). Admitted
panentheists (those who believe that the divine is present in
everything), on the other hand, abound!

I find the terms *monism* and *pantheism* to be the loose canons
of Christian apologetics. Yes, Western theology emphasizes
the transcendence of God. Yes, it has been intolerant to those
who try to balance transcendence with immanence. The
possibility that Western theology has been wrong does not
seem to cross Peters' mind. He seems content to ignore the
entire mystical heritage of Catholicism as well as such
Protestant thinkers as Paul Tillich. Also, Peters misses the
point of a great deal of New Age teaching about Jesus. Jesus is
more than a teacher or a mystic. He is the cosmic Christ, the
transformer and revivifier, and the true Self of each finite
person. Peters may not like these teachings either, but he
owes it to his readers to get the distinctions right.

The very way that Peters and many other critics of New

Age describe New Age really begs the issue. It is as if they described a dog as a speech impaired and physically handicapped biped, and then criticized the creature for not being able to speak or walk on two legs. New Age spirituality is an alternative to Christianity, and as such it should neither be described nor critiqued in Christian terms but on the basis of its own.

Peters is correct in declaring New Age naive and unrealistic. All religion, theology, and ethics share these defects. Peters sounds suspiciously like New Age when he says that "God's Spirit will transform us if by faith we seek to anticipate tomorrow's wholeness amid today's brokenness."[20] The difference between Christian theology and New Age spirituality centers in the Christian claim of an exclusive answer to human brokenness. New Age is quite aware of the gap between the way human existence is and the way it ought to be. Will any of the numerous and diverse manifestations of New Age successfully close the gap? Of course not. But neither will Peters' "if we seek to anticipate tomorrow" rhetoric.

Schultz: The Baby and the Bath Water

Ted Schultz, a onetime Aquarian visionary who is now a biologist, is another sympathetic critic of the New Age movement. He describes New Age as a blend of media invention, hype, and genuine inquiry by sincere seekers. New Age, he remarks, is "a poorly defined amalgam of exotic beliefs that range through religions, cosmologies, ethical philosophies, spiritual disciplines . . . health practices, personal-growth systems, and theories supported by psychic and paranormal claims." Despite the great diversity and undeniable inconsistency of New Age, Schultz discerns four recurrent themes that bind the movement together: (1) Western science and rationalism are responsible for most of the evil in the world; (2) there is probably no such thing as objective truth; (3) all real knowledge arises on a spiritual plane, an etheric or astral world; (4) each person is totally responsible for the conditions of his or her existence.[21] While Schultz is sympathetic to the New Age quest for personal meaning and recognizes the psychological and physical health benefits that accrue to those who adopt such New Age practices as meditation, he warns: "A strong bias toward emotion, creativity, and intuition without any attention to rationality deprives one of the ability to fully enjoy or, indeed to effectively interact with the world."[22] As he points out, science unguided by vision produces "runaway pollution, nuclear stockpiles, and all the other abuses that have made my generation so misguidedly anti-science." However, creative vision without regard for objective truth leads inexorably to "unquestioning belief in Atlantis, alien entities, reincarnation, and . . . other highly improbable superstitions."[23]

The trick, Schultz contends, is not to throw out the baby (the visionary, inner-healing, and spiritual aspects) with the bath water (the chicanery, exploitation, infantile wish-fulfillment, and the irrational). To his thinking, "the only method for separating deliberate falsities from the truth is the same as the one for separating sincere but mistaken beliefs from the truth: through a system of objective testing."[24]

Spangler's New Age Without Psychics

A major ideologist of the New Age, David Spangler, the former codirector of Scotland's Findhorn commune, offers a sober reflection on "New Age" as an introduction to *The New Age Catalogue*, a work prepared by the editors of *Body, Mind & Spirit*. Spangler muses: "What is the New Age? . . . It is the condition that emerges when I live life in a creative, empowering, compassionate manner." He adds:

> I see the New Age as a metaphor for the expression of a transformative, creative spirit. . . . I find it in the never-

ending quest to understand the nature and purpose of a God who is not just (or even primarily) the inner divinity on which so many New Age writers focus but the evocative Other whose very differences impel me to reach beyond myself and participate in the larger communion and community of life.

I see the New Age as an added dimension to our daily, ordinary living.[25]

According to Spangler, the New Age does not necessarily have anything to do with paganism, Eastern philosophies, the occult, channeling, crystals, reincarnation or psychic phenomena. True New Age consciousness, he insists, is more interested in such practical issues as restoration of the ecology, world peace, grass roots politics, planetarization (creating an awareness that we are all one people living on one world and sharing a common destiny), and issues of social justice. Although Spangler's concept of the New Age will not gain the media attention of a movie star's out-of-the-body experiences or the alleged channeled messages from a 30,000-year-old warrior, it may be of much greater significance. He argues:

> The New Age is essentially a symbol representing the human heart and intellect in partnership with God building a better world that can celebrate values of community wholeness and sacredness . . . we can forget the New Age of channels, crystals, and charisma and get on with discovering and cocreating a harmonious world that will nourish and empower all of us.[26]

It is ironic that Spangler's remarks introduce a catalogue of every imaginable form of just what Spangler wants to forget, for *Body, Mind & Spirit* (BMS)—the most widely disseminated New Age periodical, with a circulation of 170,000—is a major promoter of channelers, crystal healers, and psychics. As BMS's publisher/editor Paul Zuromski explains: "These are the tools. New Age is an idea, a way of living, a way of thinking. But how do you do New Age? You need the tools first."[27] Compare Spangler's introduction to *The New Age Catalogue* with the following brief description of its actual contents:

The New Age Catalogue: Access to Information and Sources (New York: Doubleday, Dolphin, 1988).

Price—$14.95 (paperback).

Cover art—between an overhead rainbow and a cloud below the neon outline of a man reaches upward.

Contents (in part)—
1. Intuitive development—channeling, psychic functioning, chakras/auras, crystals, astrology, numerology, tarot, palmistry, graphology, dowsing, oracles.
2. Create your reality—transformational journeys, self-help, meditation, dreamwork, astral projection/out-of-body experiences, schools, institutes, and retreats.
3. Transitions—birth, near death experiences, death and dying, reincarnation.
4. Spirituality—mystics and masters, spiritualism, women's spirituality.
5. Wholistic health and healing.
6. Bodywork—massage, acupressure, yoga, t'ai chi.
7. New Lifestyles—communities, natural products, investments, fiction, travel, music, art.
8. The Planet—global concerns, earth changes, UFOs.
9. How to order from this catalogue. All the products and services mentioned in this 244-page book may be ordered directly from *Body, Mind & Spirit.*

Terry Clifford's New Awakening

Psychiatrist Terry Clifford feels that New Age is the third of the "great awakenings" experienced in America. The first awakening was prompted by the revivalism of Jonathan Edwards. The second awakening was bifurcated. It included the millenarianism/fundamentalism of the 1840s (which, by the way, has survived in substantial institutional forms for nearly 150 years) as well as the occult/psychic/esoteric outpouring that produced Phineas Quimby, Mary Baker Eddy, the Transcendentalists, spiritualism, Madame Blavatsky's Theosophy, and the importation of Eastern gurus. It also included homegrown visionaries and eccentrics such as Guy Ballard, Daddy Grace, and Krishna Venta (whose mission ended rather abruptly when he was blown up by a dynamite bomb planted by some of his dissatisfied followers).

Writing in 1976, Clifford found America to be in the midst of yet another awakening, somehow coincident with the Bicentennial. However, she is vague as to its forms. So rather than describe or predict the third awakening, she gushes ecstatically of an imminent "quantum leap forward . . . into the vast and pristine space of self-awareness, into the clarity, ease, and energy of self-liberation—into the Spiritual Revolution of '76."[28] She would have been more accurate if she had predicted another renewal of the bifurcated awakening, for once again, the appearance of the triumph of revivalism has given way to the appearance of a resurrection of New Thought. The fact is that religious excitement of any kind will kindle New Age manifestations. Shakers, Spiritualists, and other religious innovators have often benefited from the openness, curiosity, self-dissatisfaction, and social turmoil left behind in the wake of evangelical revivals and awakenings. Once attention has been turned away from the mundane, secular, and commonplace toward the mysterious, eternal, and ecstatic, there is no going back. Even the Bible is no protection against outbreaks of mystical, panentheistic, polytheistic religiosity. In the hands of the imaginative visionary, the Bible can be made to support anything from Swedenborgianism to UFOs, from communion with departed spirits to developing psychic powers. Despite what fundamentalist foes of New Age think, every manifestation of New Age thinking for three hundred years has found a basis in the Bible and in the Bhagavad Gita and in the Koran and in whatever other holy books have been available.

Whether fundamentalism or New Age has attained anything more substantial than media visibility is not clear. What is evident is that there is a vast gulf between New Age the *perspective* and New Age the *popular mass movement.* And neither New Agers nor their critics have paid it sufficient heed.

CHAPTER TWO

New Age Forever

Somehow the question of what New Age is and whether it is really new at all reminds me of the telegram the late film star Cary Grant received from a newspaper editor. "How old Cary Grant?" the terse message read. The actor's reply: "Old Cary Grant fine. How you?"

The Roots of New Age

New Age was and is and is yet to be. It is as old as its most serious competitor, revivalism, which has waxed and waned and waxed again since erudite Jonathan Edwards terrorized the godless prior to the American Revolution, reading "Sinners in the Hands of an Angry God" with his manuscript in one hand and a blazing candle held aloft in the other. New Age began quietly and inauspiciously no one knows where or when. Perhaps it came to life in America when a few girls in Salem Village in the Massachusetts Bay Colony studied the folk spells and lore of a former slave from Barbados, or when Mother Ann Lee and her handful of followers (known as "Shakers") arrived in New York City and soon set off an explosion of ecstatic singing, dancing, and sexless communal-ism based on continuing special messages from heaven. Maybe it started when a teenaged plague victim recovered from what we would today call a near death experience in 1776 and commenced to serve as a channel of the Spirit of Life from God, calling herself "The Publick Universal Friend." Should an account of New Age begin with a handful of New Englanders who became fascinated by Hinduism in the 1820s and 1830s? Or with the poets and philosophers of the Transcendentalist movement, who combined idealism, romanticism, and what they knew of Oriental spirituality? Robert S. Ellwood, Jr., says of the Transcendentalists:

> To interpret, and find spiritual ways of living with, the new fact which was democratic and progressive in America—an America intoxicated with the ideas of change, expansion, and a brighter tomorrow—Transcendentalists looked not to Calvinism, Lockeanism, Deism, the nation's direct intellectual antecedents. It searched out instead subtler and more ancient doctrines which could give wider meaning to the new experience: the divine in all persons, the universe in all its parts, timeless motifs enacted in the historical dramas of the present, intuition rather than reason the tool for confronting events and key to the universe, contemplative retirement the mainspring of truly significant action.[1]

New Thought

Whenever and wherever New Age first sprang up, by the end of the nineteenth century it had matured in the movements known as "New Thought," whose proponents dabbled in mesmerism, faith healing, prosperity thinking, and metaphysics while looking to the Bible as the chief source of guidance. Although fellow New Englanders of the Jonathan Edwards bent would find most of her musings heretical, Mary Baker Eddy, who founded Christian Science in 1879, is typical of New Thought leaders in at least one respect: She offered her innovative way of life to humanity in the form of an interpretation of the Scriptures.

Unity School of Christianity, founded by Charles and Myrtle Fillmore, whose eclecticism makes Christian liberals look like bigots and whose looseknit polity makes Congregationalists seem autocratic, is another group that has been New Age for exactly a century. Divine Science, founded by sisters Nona and Fannie James, is a year older; and the United Church of Religious Science was established by Ernest Holmes more than seventy years ago.

The first congress of New Thought groups was held in 1894; and the National New Thought Alliance, founded in 1908, is today headquartered in Hollywood, California. Influenced heavily by Plato, Swedenborg, Hegel, Hinduism, and Transcendentalism, the Alliance in 1916 declared its purpose as follows: "To teach the infinitude of the Supreme One, the Divinity of Man and his Infinite Possibilities through the creative power of constructive thinking and obedience to the voice of the indwelling Presence which is our source of Inspiration, Power, Health, and Prosperity." From the beginning, the principal teachings of New Thought have included:

> The immanence of God, the divine nature of man, the immediate availability of God's power to man, the spiritual character of the universe, and the fact that sin, human disorders, and human disease are basically matters of incorrect thinking. . . . Man can live in oneness with God in love, truth, peace, health, and plenty.[3]

New Age not only adopts the precepts of New Thought, but it also calls on the doctrines of scores of organized, not-so-organized, and even disorganized sects. It derives channeling from the "trance mediumship" of Spiritualism, the most pervasive and influential manifestation of Anglo-Saxon cultural or folk religion of the last century, with a dash of Native American shamanism thrown in for good measure. In *The Encyclopedia of American Religions,* J. Gordon Melton describes no fewer than 312 groups belonging to "the metaphysical family" (31 New Thought Groups and 5 forms of Christian Science) and to "the psychic and New Age family" (Swedenborgian groups, spiritualism, teaching spiritualism, theosophy, Alice Bailey groups, liberal Catholicism, the I AM movement, miscellaneous theosophical groups, Rosicrucians, other occult groups, drug-oriented groups, flying saucer groups, other New Age groups, ritual magick, witchcraft, neo-paganism, and satanism).[4] Although such groups tend to be loosely structured, volatile, and transitory, many have endured for decades.[5]

The Religion of the Hippies

Only a few years ago, New Age spirituality found expression in the psychedelic movement. For many of us, our encounters with the Flower Children (or perhaps being Flower Children) constituted "the dawning of the Age of Aquarius." The Hippies were many things: a youth crusade, a media creation, a movement of social protest and antiwar activism, an alternative life-style with its own weird costuming and tribal rites, a collection of clichés and gibberish, and, in some ways, a movement of spiritual renewal. For many of the Hippies, the use of the powerful hallucinogenic, lysergic acid diethylamide (LSD) was sacramental, a mystical experience, a leaving behind of mundane reality and an entering into the realm of transcendent bliss. In the words of one observer:

> The movement is composed of people who have taken LSD and/or other hallucinogens and see in these drugs a tool for bringing about changes which they deem desirable. The emphasis is on the enhancement of inner experience and on the development of hidden personal resources. It is an *optimistic* doctrine, for it holds that there are power and greatness concealed within everyone. It is an *intellectual* doctrine, for it values experience and understanding [the proper interpretation of experience] more than action and

visible change. It concerns itself with areas dear to the thinker: art, philosophy, religion, and the nature and potentials of man. It is a *mystical* doctrine, for it prizes illumination and a unified world view with meaning beyond that drawn from empirical reality. It is a *realistic* doctrine as well, for it counsels compromise and accommodation between the inner and outer worlds. . . . And it is, explicitly, a *revolutionary* doctrine, although the revolution it proposes is internal, psychological and by no means novel. It calls for freedom from internal constraints, freedom to explore one's self and the cosmos, and the freedom to use LSD and other drugs as the means thereto.[6]

Ingestion of LSD produces an eight- to twelve-hour "trip," characterized by profound changes in thought, mood, and activity. Like all intense experiences, an acid trip can bear a variety of interpretations. If trippers were disciples of Christ before tripping, they may have visions of the Trinity, the Virgin, or the Last Judgment. If they were students of Vedanta or Zen Buddhism, their visions may be distinctively Oriental. Tiny, a friend of mine who was the archetypal Hippie, was disenchanted with both the Catholicism of his youth and the depersonalization of humankind in a greed-motivated, technological society. He pursued an Eastern vision of wholeness without "having gained the stability, maturity, and elasticity needed to assimilate the Eastern values."[7] For Tiny, Oriental spirituality was a refuge that, because no one understood it sufficiently, no one was able to refute. It was not so much that his experience demanded Eastern categories as that Tiny's chosen psychedelic gurus depended heavily on them.

In some of Tiny's experiences, the elements of bliss, sensual wonder, "awareness and reality," and awe predominated. At other times, feelings of terror, rejection, and apprehension were paramount. Under the guidance of Hippie gurus, the drug-induced state was interpreted as the attainment of a mystical vision of ultimate reality. LSD was used to still ordinary consciousness and enable the individual to step outside of himself. Normal consciousness and the habitual subconscious associations of a lifetime were thereby suspended.

During the late 1960s and early 1970s, I was intrigued by Tiny and those like him who seemed to pursue "a high-minded search for union with deity."[8] Tiny was a true believer. What did he believe? Strict standards of behavior governed his life. What were they? When I attempted to answer these questions, I encountered grave difficulties, for, as is the case with most mystical religions, experience and not information were considered of utmost importance. According to Tiny, the psychedelic experience transcends every symbol, concept, or explanation. A reverent respect was demanded for the ineffability of both the awareness achieved and the presence disclosed through this experience. Tiny ransacked the congenial mystical traditions of the Orient— Upanishadic Hinduism, esoteric Taoism, Zen Buddhism— for expressions of experiences that rupture the categories of the religious orthodoxies of the West. Because the Catholicism of his youth had lost contact with its own mystical heritage, Tiny explained, the priests who had served his parish had answered his requests for the bread of ecstatic experience with the stones of irrelevant religious doctrines.

For Tiny, the discovery and actualization of one's true self was the way, the truth, and the life. The "chief end of man" to him was the progressive realization of one's unique selfhood, in his argot, "doing your own thing." Once again he resorted to Eastern spirituality to express his basic intuition. He affirmed that the same divine presence that reveals itself as being, consciousness, and bliss in the psychedelic experience is the ground of all beings, the very core of each human personality. As the Hindu Upanishads proclaim, the Atman (true self) and Brahman (the divine spirit) are one. Each person is a never-to-be-repeated image of the hidden one, a unique and cherished reflection of the unitary being, which

underlies all things. Thus Tiny was a "mystical panenth-
eist"—that is, he attempted to realize in the celebration of
each person's distinctiveness the ultimate harmony upon
which all differences are based, the universal spirit present in
all things as the bearer of joy and meaning.

Tiny was deeply committed to astrology—an aspect of his
belief that the divine is present fully in all things. I will always
cherish the lengthy and detailed astrological analysis he
prepared of me—his teacher the model Pisces—replete with
sun sign, moon sign, and rising star. As I am a traditional
Westerner with a sense of responsibility for the transformation of my environment, Tiny's interest in astrology struck
me as a shirking of his accountability for his own actions. I
often accused him of having found in the stars what my
generation formerly found in Freudianism—an inscrutable
determinism that can be blamed for every misfortune,
whether self-inflicted or circumstantial. But Tiny's astrology
was much more than arcane fortune-telling. It was the
expression of a participation in the unity of all things. He
often asked me to look at it from his point of view—if reality is
a seamless whole, an essential harmony in which every part
affects and is affected by every other part, then human beings
cannot be unaffected by the stars and planets. To Tiny,
astrology was not so much a science as a reaffirmation of the
fundamental oneness of reality.

He often told me that he belonged to an international
movement, a community of communities—each different
from its counterpart; yet each an embodiment of identical
values. Tiny was never content to reject the conventions of
American life. In their place, he had found an all-embracing
style of life, a supportive fellowship or tribe that shared his
ideals, his aspirations, and, above all, his religious experience.

The Hippie concern for community initially grew from a
regard for where, when, and with whom you trip. The
importance of preparation received an emphasis similar to
the matter of purification in the rites of primitive religions.

Inadequate preparation for the psychedelic experience was
considered foolhardy from the beginning of the psychedelic
movement.

As we have noted, an important aspect of Hippie
community was the psychedelic experience, an extrovertive
mysticism that heightened sensory awareness, producing a
delight for sight, sound, odor, taste, and touch that far
outlasted the LSD trip. The Hippie rediscovered the body
and its senses. The Hippies also found that mind, body, and
spirit are inseparable, that the healing of one requires the
reintegration of all. Hence, the Hippies turned away from
modern medicine and looked to folk remedies, herbs, floral
essences, organically grown foods (free of carcinogens,
additives, preservatives, herbicides, and pesticides), massage,
acupuncture, reflexology, and chiropractic as tools of
"holistic health." Some Hippies adopted the names and
ceremonies of Native Americans, finding a dreamlike vision
of what the Hippies themselves sought in accounts of
medicine men's hallucinogenically induced trance states,
reverence for nature, and tribal solidarity. In some places,
alternative health clinics—offering a smorgasbord of non-
traditional services—flourished, fought the disdain of the
medical establishment, and eventually faded away because
everyone wanted to be a guru and no one could be bothered
to balance the books, take out the garbage, or distinguish
between unconventional and irresponsible.

Inner Space, the first monthly "magazine of the Psychedelic
community," spawned more than fifty underground newspapers, which served Hippiedom as an outlet for creative (and
often obscene) energies, while fulfilling the usual functions
of the press. In such publications, one found news coverage,
advice to the lovelorn and drug-worn, letters to the editors,
advertisements of products and services of special interest to
the Hippie market, and so on. The Hippie free press
movement was but another example of a striving after
solidarity. Hippiedom was not content to reject American

conventionality. In its place Hippies offered what they considered a viable alternative, an all-embracing style of life. Hippies desired a community that permitted each to "do his or her own thing" within a supportive social structure in which values, ideals, aspirations, and, above all, religious experience and spiritual perspective were shared.

What became of the psychedelic movement? The Hippie was replaced by the pseudo-Hippie, the plastic Hippie, the weekend Hippie, and the adolescent Hippie. Hippies left the scene, and the thrill- and pleasure-seekers took their place. The hedonistic cults came to the center of the stage; the dance got wilder, but there were few social ideas (or ideas of any kind). The music got louder, the lights more intense, but cultural revolution turned into MTV, CDs, and multi-million-dollar worldwide tours.

Many erstwhile dropouts burned out and became Jesus Freaks or Hare Krishnas or Moonies or Rajneeshies or TM enthusiasts. Many went back into the mainstream, sadder but wiser, wanting a life not very different from that of their parents after all, even though the tastes, values, and expectations of these returnees remained just different enough to make their parents uncomfortable with them.

The Hippie phenomenon was a warning. It revealed the dissatisfaction of America's youth with our materialism, our hypocrisies, our toleration of mediocrity and injustice. In some measure, the Hippies expanded our minds, reawakened our senses and sensuality, and reminded us of our own hunger for the experience of a living God. I did not look for God at the end of a needle or in an acid-laced sugar cube. But because of Tiny, I looked for God not just with my intellect, but with my whole being. I felt God's presence once again pressing on me, filtering throughout my body, charging my sensations and relationships with the electricity of the Real. And I knew that I was forbidden to cry peace where there is no peace.

The Hippies were neither a fraternity of saints' nor an

assemblage of self-pitying brats—and yet they were both. The Hippies were wise and naive, idealists and cynics. They cared for one another and for the future of their world, and yet they were also incredibly reckless and irresponsible. Their doctrine was optimistic, intellectual, mystical, and revolutionary. Unfortunately, most of them were not.

Hippiedom is a long time gone. Hounded by the authorities, terrorized by thugs, victimized by the unscrupulous, disoriented by the drug-induced ecstasy through which they sought the shattering and reintegrating intensity characteristic of all genuine religious experience—the "love generation" melted away. In the meantime, we all got bored with counterculture—with Hippies, Yippies, and student activists. It simply went out of style. Even those who survived their own Hippie days with intact bodies and reasonably functioning minds got tired of scrounging to survive and of changing mates and identities the way that others of us changed our socks.

My Hippie friends of twenty years ago are now grandparents. They hold professional jobs or are entrepreneurs. They are married or divorced. They drive Volvos and Subarus. They own homes. And yet they are not just like their never-anything-but-straight neighbors. Hippiedom is not as dead as it may appear. Their questions remain, and their influence continues, many of their number living on and laboring on as mainstays of the New Age. Replace drug-induced mysticism with new forms of ecstasy. Retain the beliefs in the power and greatness concealed within each person, the positive regard for experience and understanding, the pursuit of illumination and a unified world view, and the longing for a revolution of consciousness. Add the quest for community, the tying together of questing individuals, teachers, leaders, and service providers through a substantial alternative press/computer bulletin board network, and the Hippie community of yesterday reemerges.

The Lure of New Age

A reading of the media, as well as of mainline and conservative critics of New Age, gives one the impression that there has suddenly sprung up a vast, silly, weird, and novel hodgepodge, which is being foisted on the unwary and credulous by greedy charlatans. How vast New Age is, I cannot say. Most New Age practices do not require that one join a distinctively New Age church or sect—although some do offer membership. But often such membership is nonexclusive. Hence, one can be a member of a local Unity Church and still be a Presbyterian. The weirdness and silliness of New Age is largely a matter of perception and point of view—although it is hard to take seriously everything published, sold, or otherwise promoted as New Age. But then again, who can swallow all the folk customs, periodicals, radio and TV messages, gospel tracts, glowing statues, medallions, get-rich-quick schemes, and guaranteed miracles promoted within organized, not-so-organized, and disorganized forms of Christianity?

New Age may be a hodgepodge, but it is scarcely novel. It was not born yesterday. Under the New Age umbrella, one finds a plethora of groups with histories, traditions, liturgies, literatures, and distinctive ways of life. It may be a jumble, but it is a vital and living jumble, and like all such tumultuous muddles it attracts the sincere as well as the unsavory, the wise as well as the imbecilic, the well intentioned as well as the self-serving. It is not a spiritual blight, a fungus among us that flourishes when the divine light is eclipsed. It is not a kind of disease that surfaces now and then when orthodox faith in God has gone into decline. New Age has been around for a long, long time, and it will continue to be around as long as it serves the real needs of real human beings.

Ten years ago, Martin E. Marty called attention to a plethora of works, written by his fellow American religious historians, that had such titles as *Strange Sects and Curious*

Cults, The New Religions, and *Faith for the Few.* Marty sternly chastised the authors of these books:

> No one chartered them to put narrow boundaries around their story or their subjects; these authors simply reflected the viewpoints of their sponsors and clienteles, and thus unofficially established certain faiths as non-strange or non-curious because they seemed old and belonged to the many.[9]

Established religions, with their formal creeds and implicit or explicit views of acceptable behavior uphold the normative values of society. In both mainline and evangelical forms, established religions undergird society and, in return, receive society's respect and approbation. Compared to the religious establishment, small deviant groups seem unconventional, aberrant, oddball, and uncouth.

Such groups attract those who feel different, out of harmony, and not at home in the mainstream. They appeal to those looking for solace and self-understanding. In their own view, such seekers are more self-conscious, sensitive, special, complex, and aware than the rest of humanity.[10] Marching to a different drummer, they are out of step even with those closest to them. The psychics and gurus I know are wellsprings of guidance and hope to thousands; yet, they seem unable to find happiness in their own personal lives. My friend Emma, who works at a major New Age bookstore, claims that, almost without exception, the best-sellers of New Age are written by divorced or unhappily married persons. She explains that divorce has become the rite of passage for human beings in the late twentieth century, that until a seeker has gone through the initiatory stage of suffering and purification, represented by divorce, he or she cannot attain enlightenment.

The appeal of New Age has always been to the marginal—to those who do not or cannot fit in, who sometimes struggle for decades to discover a sense of vocation and mission, whose lives are always on the threshold of fulfillment, but who never fully enter in. For such seekers, relates Joseph Campbell, "The adventure is its own reward—but it's necessarily dangerous, having both negative and positive possibilities, all of them beyond control."[11]

All the New Age rhetoric about making one's own reality masks the experience of many New Agers, who feel that they are helpless to resist forces that rule their lives—forces of economics, prejudice, racism, ageism, and sexism, over which they exercise no control. The strident insistence that each of us creates his or her own world gives utterance to the desperation of the marginal and the powerless—particularly of women, who today comprise 70 to 90 percent of the New Age market.

Historically and in our own day, New Age redresses women's age-old grievances against traditional religions, which banish the feminine principle and worship a male deity. New Age condemns the religious establishment for relegating women to the roles of breeders of men's children, supporters of men's work, and auxiliaries in male-directed worship. Instead of repressing the feminine, New Age offers spiritualities in which women are dominant in number and influence, religions that accord the feminine major significance in their mythical expressions of the nature of the divine. New Age is a return to the primal and archaic state of religious expression in which "woman magic and earth magic are the same"[12]—a state of being replete with ecstasy, possession, vision, prophecy, and healing arts. As Ellwood observes, the predominance of women in mystical and healing cults "is a worldwide fact . . . evident in Haitian voodoo, the ancient Greek Dionysiacs, and the Japanese new religions, as in the somewhat more decorous Shakers, Spiritualists, Theosophists, and Pentecostalists of America."[13]

Women turn to New Age for many reasons: to find the power denied to them in the patriarchal religious institutions

of the West and in the patriarchal systems of domination that
such institutions have long underwritten; because the mythic
structure of New Age is better suited to their role as mothers
and nurturers than the metaphors and stories about women
found in the Bible; and because they are comfortable in New
Age, which is largely of, by, and for women. Finally, women
flock to New Age spirituality as a refuge from the
disappointments of romantic love and sexuality. Rather than
depending on some man to support, fulfill, excite, and
provide them with their sense of identity—the criticism many
feminists and New Agers make of traditional marriage
arrangements—New Age women seek the power to be whole,
loving, and healing within themselves.

As they pursue their idiosyncratic light, New Agers—men
as well as women—are surprised to find themselves regarded
as crazy, confused, misguided, or charlatans by those who, in
their eyes, have never known anything but darkness. To the
seeker and to the seeker's critics, the seeker's values,
attitudes, and patterns of behavior seem novel, but the
newness is usually in the eye of the beholder. As Ellwood
explains:

> An emergent religion . . . is one which appears suddenly
> and unexpectedly, and which stands out from the sea of
> established religion like a new volcanic island or a rock
> revealed by an unusually low tide. Though it may be a result of
> an understandable process and even something which in a
> sense was there all along, it gives an appearance of novelty and
> striking contrast to the established faiths that surround it.[14]

Comparing New Age groups, tendencies, and influences to
established religions is like comparing the amoeba to the
whale. As Ellwood notes, these ephemeral entities are "tiny,
short-lived, continually dividing, yet in one sense far more
immortal."[15] While the structures of established religions are
stable, those of New Age groups are protean and flexible.
Mainstream churches are like families—necessary, depend-

able, a refuge that one may count on. New Age spirituality is more like falling in love—it is impassioned, irrational, subject to wild alterations in mood, and impossible to sustain. Its potential for personal creativity and its proclivity for interpersonal destructiveness are inseparable. As with love, seeking does not guarantee finding; neither does deliberate avoidance nor indifference provide immunity.

Established religion and New Age complement and fulfill each other. Yet, neither is completely comfortable with or trusting of the other. Further, while New Age tolerates and accepts the contribution of the establishment, the establishment would prefer to see New Age packed and on the first boat to a faraway country. Since the establishment has greater influence on the media, education, and the government, it gets to call names. That is why New Age is described as "odd," "eccentric," "bizarre," and "dangerous."

New Age Defined

Are New Age groups different enough to threaten established religions? The answer to this question will define just what New Age is. Yes, indeed, New Age is dangerous, a menace to unexamined assumptions. From their inception before the American Revolutionary War until this very day, the seekers, visionaries, and mystics have urged such unsettling novelties as the following.

New Age is panentheistic instead of theistic. To its foes, and even to some of its adherents, it often appears pantheistic. Established religion fears that panentheism worships the creation instead of its Creator, replaces obedience to moral law with preoccupation with self-realization, and short-circuits social action by diverting attention away from the evil of the present world and toward the quest for quiescent mystical states.

New Age is spiritually ecological. It approaches nature as a manifestation of the divine rather than as separated from a

transcendent God by an unbridgeable gulf. Theistic religion
acts as though nature exists to be exploited, controlled, or
killed. New Age emphasizes the inseparability and mutual
dependence of humankind and nature. Its panentheistic
reverence for life places it in opposition to such capitalistic
commonplaces as the exploitation and despoiling of the
environment for the sake of short-term profits, the indifference to the needs of the individual and the family in the
modern workplace.

New Age is reflective. It emphasizes the need for self-understanding through meditation. If the divine is present within
the self as its true essence, the individual must learn to
discriminate between the chatter of his or her own
personality and the still, small voice of God within.
Established religion prefers conceiving of God as "out there"
to be communicated with through prayer and ritual.

New Age is transformative rather than reformative. Established
religion measures spiritual success in quantitative terms: the
number of souls saved, of edifices constructed, of hospitals
built, of schools opened, and so on. New Age is more
concerned with the transformation of consciousness. A
televangelist who is a notorious New Age baiter demanded of
Witches on "The Oprah Winfrey Show" a few years ago:
"What has your religion ever done for the world? Where are
your hospitals? Your universities?" As a movement of
revitalization, New Age is really not that different from
historic revivalism. It attempts to change persons first and
leaves it to transformed persons to change the world. *World* is
really the key word, for the reunification of human beings
with their environment and the rescuing of that environment
from destruction are central to New Age. In responding to
the question of where their institutions are, the Witches and
their allies should have responded, "You are living in it!"

New Age is androgynous. New Age, as we have seen,
promotes the importance of the feminine aspects of the real
and the authority of women. It is threatening to those who

can accept the feminine aspects of neither their own personalities nor of the divine; and to those who insist that women must remain in subordinate roles within the family, society, and the church. However, it does not replace male dominance with female dominance.

New Age is xenophilic, in love with the strange and alien; the establishment is xenophobic. It represents a reorientation away from the dominant values, attitudes, and mores and toward alternatives that are found in distant and remote cultures. For better or worse, the imagination of New Age is riveted to the far away, to the spatially and temporally alien, to other civilizations and worlds, to past lives and parallel dimensions, to higher planes and superhuman beings. Traditional religion is frightened by the new and the strange. American culture is totemistic, prone to confuse its values and attitudes with God's will. Inside is familiar and secure. The alien (cultures, peoples, languages, or religions) is confusing, unsettling, and frightening. Such fear readily turns to anger, hatred, and persecution.

New Age is ecstatic. It values the out-of-the-ordinary, the sensational, the unusual. It thrives on novelty, is open to the exploration of the limits of human consciousness, and celebrates the transpersonal and psychic dimensions of human existence. New Age is committed to pursuing sources of knowledge that transcend both sensory data and logic. It is concerned with dreams, visions, and imagination. Mainstream religion emphasizes the cozy familiarity of its traditions, doctrines, and mores. Fundamentalism reacts to New Age as though evangelicals had a monopoly on religious euphoria. Christian charismatics are profoundly troubled by New Age because it provides direct competition, for similar phenomena (healing, deliverance from possession, receiving messages from above, and the like) occur in both settings. In addition, the dominant secular humanistic mind-set rejects ecstatic manifestations as unscientific, illogical, and antisocial.

New Age is life-affirming and death-denying. It is expressive rather than repressive. It is afraid of neither imagination nor inspiration. It maintains that death, disease, poverty, and suffering do not speak the final word about the destiny of the individual or of humankind. It is more interested in human possibilities than in limitations, the realization of the Christ-nature rather than preoccupation with sinfulness.

New Age is tolerant of the mainstream. It is open, accepting, and nonjudgmental, even uncritical. Its foes see it as relativistic, polytheistic, and senseless. It is inclusivistic, accepting the Christ and the Buddha and Zen masters and Sufi sages and Hindu swamis and Native American shamans and renamed New Yorkers with Asian-sounding names. It does not insist that one must cease to be a Roman Catholic or a Protestant or a Jew.

For the most part, New Age is even tolerant of New Age. Unlike the mainstream in general and fundamentalism in particular, New Age can forgive, overlook, laugh at, and even enjoy its charlatans, con artists, manipulators, adulterers, and money grubbers. There is a powerful New Age impulse to absorb corruption without itself being polluted. For New Age, the origin of evil is error rather than rebellion. The primal form of error is egocentricity, the belief in the ultimate significance of the separate self. New Age can laugh at itself when its gurus, guides, and teachers forget who they are and begin to think that money, power, and sex are of any importance. One can learn many valuable lessons from a crackpot, a clown, a madman or madwoman, or a seducer. It is rather like the Roman Catholic theology of the Eucharist: The sacrament depends on the presence of God—not on the intelligence or ethical purity of the celebrant.

New Age, Power, and Charisma

New Age can laugh at the media when they confuse the road map with the landscape and begin wagging fingers at

the all too human foibles of God-intoxicated human beings.
Religion is the discovery of absolute power and the opening
of oneself to its demands. Lord Acton was right: "Power
tends to corrupt and absolute power corrupts absolutely."
(There is also wisdom in the anonymous quotation: "Power
can corrupt, but absolute power is absolutely delightful.")
And the concrete expressions of power in human affairs
often include money, sex, and interpersonal influence.
Persons who deal in power—as its instruments or media—
often abuse money, sex, and interpersonal influence. That
does not discredit power, for power is neither good nor evil.
It just is, and it attracts. Jesus lost his temper, accepted
valuable gifts from one or more of his followers, associated
with prostitutes and other despised elements of society; yet,
he remained for Christians the one without sin. The power of
his person, the power of which he was custodian and
expression, attracts men and women two thousand years
after his earthly career.

I have known a few New Age gurus. Virtually without
exception, they have violated the ethical rules by which I try
to live my life. Some of them have violated the rules by which
they insist others should live their lives. I do not particularly
want them for friends or house guests—let alone as teachers
and examples. But that is because I cannot see through them
or beyond them. Their devotees can. These gurus have
become symbols in the minds of their followers, so powerful
that they turn the stable inner lives of their disciples into
chaos and turn the chaos into kaleidoscopic patterns of new
meaning and satisfaction.

Charisma is the meeting of objective characteristics and
subjective needs. The more intensely dissatisfied individuals
are, the more they will project on the mysterious other (be it
loved one, star, candidate, deity, ecstatic experience, or
movement) those qualities found lacking in themselves. Is it
necessary for there to be "something there," some basis for
the projection? I used to think so. Today I am not so sure.

Believers rely on a peculiar alchemy that not only turns lead into gold, but it turns used Kleenex into gold as well.

For nearly three centuries, this second stream of American religious experience has flowed alongside the main channel, sometimes touching it and mingling forms and contents, sometimes remaining at a distance. Being narrower, the second stream flows swifter, hence such innovations as equality of the sexes and the staggering number of female charismatic leaders. Since most of its meanderings are far beneath the surface of individual consciousness or public awareness, it is unknown until it surfaces or until the observer plunges into the depths to find it. But it is always there.

CHAPTER THREE

New Age Comes to the Magazine Racks

The New Age Journal

It was the worst summer since the dust-bowl years of the Great Depression. The temperature in our room in the red brick dormitory at Episcopal Divinity School was about 140° during the day and 100° at night. The humidity was so palpable that it could be chewed. Our only salvation, the air-conditioned library, failed us. The compressor died. I continued writing in the hermetically sealed library, but I felt entombed in a sauna. On a terribly unpleasant June afternoon, my wife and I made our way in a taxicab with a broken air conditioner to the offices of *New Age Journal* in Brighton, Massachusetts, about two miles from where we were staying in Cambridge.

The *Journal,* important not only for its content and leadership role, but also because its very name celebrates the emergence of the New Age, is located—quite ironically—behind a McDonald's and above a fur and leather goods business. We were greeted by Jonathan Adolph, a longtime staffer who is now senior editor. Jon is in his late twenties, is slim, of medium height, and has dark brown hair and a neatly trimmed beard. We had previously conversed via telephone, Jon having interviewed me for an article on a West Coast guru who was accused of sexually exploiting his followers.

As befits an editor and writer, Jon is fluent, articulate, and familiar with contemporary literature. Jon sees New Age as two distinct (but less than separate) entities. "New Age," he says, "is both a philosophy and a marketplace." He adds, "The essence of the philosophy is real decentralization. New Age does not rely on figures of authority." As Jon sees it, New

Age is based on the recognition that our society is sick, but that it can be healed. The symptoms of the disease include our vast investment in "the war machine," the despoiling of the environment, the oppression of women and minorities by a white male patriarchal power structure, and the way we continue to kill ourselves by being out of harmony with nature, inviting into our systems all manner of stress-related symptoms and diseases, such as cancer and AIDS.

"What this society needs," Jon offered, "is a shift of consciousness, a shift in the way it sees itself, a returning to what is natural. And that's what is happening as more and more people question traditional assumptions about life, the future of the planet, and the nature of reality." The new paradigm of reality, which Marilyn Ferguson has expounded in her "landmark book" *The Aquarian Conspiracy*, "sees humankind embedded in nature . . . as stewards of all our resources, inner and outer. It says we are not victims, not pawns, not limited by conditions or conditioning."[1] Jon is convinced that our society has been more influenced than it knows by New Age perspectives. "Unfortunately the media," he complains, "is hung up on the marketing or Madison Avenue aspects of New Age"—the gurus, the quackery, and the hype. He stated: "This kind of New Age is a fad, but the ideas derived from 'the Perennial Philosophy,' from the Romantic, Transcendentalist spiritual quest are here to stay." As he envisions it, the real New Age, the New Age which is almost ashamed to call itself by this name, combines such seemingly disparate elements as "human potential, holistic health, recycling, organic foods, grassroots activism, practical spirituality, meditation, ecology, appropriate technology, feminism, and progressive politics."[2]

In *The 1988 Guide to New Age Living*, Jon has written that media coverage of New Age

> has focused primarily on the various *metaphysical* interests of those said to be new age, in particular, channeling (whereby

ancient entities allegedly speak through otherwise ordinary people) and crystals (which supposedly help the body balance and realign its "energy field"). For the many philosophers, social critics, futurists, educators, and others who have been exploring alternative, new age ideas for decades, however, these other-worldly pursuits are at most *fringe issues*— distractions from the largely practical and down-to-earth matters that lie at the center of new age thinking.[3]

Jon agrees with New Age pioneer David Spangler, who says: "The new age has little to do with prophecy or the imagination of a new world, but everything to do with the imagination to see our world in new ways that can empower us toward compassion, transformative actions and atti- tudes."[4]

Although the New Age movement is based on "spiritual awareness," it is not a religion. New Age Journal's *1988 Guide to New Age Living* offers products and services in the following categories: health and wellness; environmental, peace, and human rights groups; holistic learning centers, New Age books, transformational travel; New Age music and videos; and socially conscious investment services. But there is no category for spirituality! Indeed, the movement finds its relationship to spiritual reality "problematic and confusing." Jon is wary of "transcendental shortcuts"—relying on crystals, channeling, and psychic phenomena. He prefers a "practical spirituality," the essence of which is enlarging the sense of the sacred to include not just that which is confined within a closed religious context, but to engage in "the process of seeing the heaven that is right here on earth every day."[5] Rather than focusing on gurus and quick fixes, NAJ has presented such personal and individual practices as meditation, lucid dreaming, therapeutic prayer, and positive visualization.

On the basis of personal transformation, the individual must move out into the social arena in order to reshape the world. In the words of George Leonard and Michael

Murphy: "If the divine is present in an individual soul it must be sought and found in man's institutions as well. For people will not realize individual salvation without a saved society."[6] Jon notes that NAJ has tightened up its standards for its advertisers. These changes were made in part in response to what he and others saw as the commercialization and exploitation of New Age ways of life, and, he acknowledges, there remains a not so subtle tension between the editorial content of NAJ and it advertisements. "New Age for many," he insists, "has become instant karma, psychic pets, and crystal healing," the New Age fad rather than the New Age philosophy. Just as the counterculture degenerated into the excesses of the heavy metal rock and drug scene, so also the New Age is in danger of inducing in the public a kind of psychospiritual hangover, leaving behind only a bad, bad "morning after."

During our conversation of nearly two hours, which ebbed and flowed into many New Age tributaries and backwaters, I was struck by the centrality of Jon's notion of ecological responsibility to his descriptions of the New Age movement. He was careful to distinguish between what he terms "deep ecology," the notion that solving our environmental problems requires a change in our spiritual relationship to the earth, and "social ecology," which recognizes that the environment is out of balance primarily because of human action and social injustice.

"Another part of the New Age movement," Jon explains, "is people who are seeking new solutions to old problems." He adds, "Our attitude is, 'Let's try everything and see what works and what doesn't. But don't tell us what we can't do until we try it for ourselves.' " New Age is not a social agenda that attempts to reform society from the top down by major funding and centralized administration. New Age is the world of single individuals, many of them entrepreneurs, who "think globally and act locally."

"For instance," Jon stated, "if each of us were to raise his or her own vegetables in our back yards, we could save millions of dollars, the millions of gallons of gasoline that are used not only to cultivate produce on the farm but to transport it to market. This is just one example." Jon admits that it is not easy to be consistent. He referred to "all natural apple juice sold in non-biodegradable plastic containers" as an illustration of inconsistency.

Having been exposed to this entrepreneurial libertarianism, Jon is profoundly suspicious of "organized alternatives—centralized groups, gurus with their unnatural allegiances." He describes them as "a sign of how desperate we are."

For Jon, *New Age Journal* exists as an agency of regeneration and renewal, "a socially healing magazine." Begun in November of 1974 as a voice of the counterculture, a Hippie publication, its staff was former members of *East-West Magazine*. Originally called *The New Journal* (but copyrighted as *The New Journal of Planetary Culture*), after one issue it was renamed *New Age Journal* at the suggestion of a local book publisher, who remembered an English publication of the same name. Florence Grave, former editor and associate publisher of NAJ maintains: "Our magazine . . . was named fourteen years ago after a London newspaper founded in the early 1900s by A. H. Orage. Orage's New Age was known for publishing leading-edge thinking by some of his time's most forward-looking writers such as Ezra Pound and Upton Sinclair."[7]

Early issues of the reborn NAJ featured such counterculture stars as Beat poet Alan Ginsburg and shamanism chronicler Carlos Castaneda. The September 1976 issue included a comprehensive spiritual history of America, referred to on the cover as "Saints & Lunatics," but actually entitled "The Master List" by Terry Clifford. The July-August 1976 issue's cover article dealt with the presidential bid of California's governor, Jerry Brown.

In the early 1980s, the magazine became "hip" rather than

"Hippie." Articles on rock and roll, t'ai chi, and high tech were prominent. The September 1983 issue launched "the 'new' New Age." Jon explains: "The tone became zippier. We went to the four color, slick paper, and nicely laid out magazine that it is today. It might be said that this was our 'Golden Age.' " In the next phase of its history, Jon relates, the magazine attempted to broaden its appeal, becoming "less counterculture and more mainstream."

NAJ's circulation leveled off at about 120,000. A large staff and the expenses of monthly publication could not be supported by the subscriptions, newsstand sales, and advertisers, so in July of 1986 the staff, including Adolph, was fired. But shortly thereafter, NAJ reemerged as a bimonthly with a pared-down staff. The explosion of New Age book titles made it much easier to fill its pages with excerpts. Interest grew, and circulation, it is claimed, has increased to about 150,000.

Reflections on NAJ

Many of the religions I have studied over the years have both philosophical/moralistic and popular/irrational/amoral manifestations—the two elements often in conflict. The philosophically inclined adherent sees the popular manifestations as gross and preliminary, but necessary. The divine, says the philosopher, seeks and finds human beings where they are. The fanatic devotee simply ignores the philosopher, not really caring what he says. In his heart, the devotee knows what his god requires, and no association of trained priests or guild of educated theologians can tell him otherwise. My visit to *New Age Journal* made me aware of just how deeply the New Age movement is split. Jon and his constituency represent the philosophical/moralistic side of New Age. They are its ethicists, theologians, and guardians. In them, the idealism of the counterculture lives on—Hippiedom meets Yuppiedom, and in the meeting both are essentially transformed. The

Hippie finds that he or she is in this world after all; the Yuppie that he or she is not essentially or permanently of this world.

In the NAJ version of the movement, New Age combines passion, life-style, and a vision of social transformation. However, where it all comes from is not clear. Is there an underlying mystical perception of the Real, a sense of oneness with nature? It is hard to answer. Whether NAJ has the horsepower to actualize that vision remains to be seen. In protecting itself against the gurus, the psychics, and the crystal channelers, has NAJ cut itself off from the energizing particularity of popular New Age? Are the bread and circuses of popular New Age not the jumping-off point without which few begin the journey? Is there any choice but to risk exposure to the New Age fad with all its wild extravagance? Don't we all need the "tools"?

Body, Mind & Spirit

Providence, Rhode Island, is a pleasant ninety-minute drive from Cambridge—just long enough to examine one's preconceptions and develop an open mind. On a cool (at last!), clear June morning, I was on my way to the offices of *Body, Mind & Spirit*, probably the most widely circulated New Age magazine. I was taking my prejudices with me. BMS is just too weird, too low-level popular, too uncritical for my taste, what with its UFO abductee stories, its up-to-the-minute channeled messages from Seth (whose "official" medium, Jane Roberts, passed from this earthly plane some time ago), and its full page ads for JZ Knight (who channels "Ramtha the Enlightened One . . . the most celebrated spiritual teacher of the 80s").

I had phoned Paul Zuromski a week earlier. Our appointment had been delayed by the birth of his third child and his need to be at home. He had asked me if I had seen the *New Age Catalogue*, which he and the staff of BMS had written.

Indeed I had, I told him, and I had mentioned the discrepancy I perceived between the introduction by David Spangler (who insists that New Age is not psychics, channelers, and gurus), and the text of the catalogue (full of psychics, channelers, and gurus). I stated that this gap was a major focus in my thinking about New Age. Paul declared: "No one's approached New Age that way. I'll be interested in what you have to say, and I'd certainly like to talk to you."

"The gap" was our first topic of discussion. Pointing to a copy of the catalogue, Paul asserted: "These are tools. New Age is an idea, a way of living, a way of thinking. But how do you do it? You need the tools. And psychics, channelers, and gurus *are* some of the tools." For Paul, the catalogue sets the boundaries. It separates good New Age from bad New Age. If something or someone is in the catalogue, that means, Paul stated, that "we have tested them and found them to be O.K."

Paul's tendency is to make an emphatic assertion and then back away from it. For example, after stating that "we have found them to be O.K.," he added, "Of course, not everyone agrees." He frequently boasted of how well BMS and the *New Age Catalogue* were doing, but wondered aloud if the success would last. Paul is very proud of what he has accomplished, but does not want to tempt the gods with his hubris.

"We're all explorers," Paul added. Unlike some New Agers who are trying to transform social consciousness, Paul is committed to "changing everybody individually—to change the inner person." "We're not journalists," he explained. "We're not trying to report objectively on everything that's happening in New Age. Rather we're saying: 'Here are some interesting options. Consider them. But you have to make your own decision.'"

Although it became clear in our conversation that BMS is an outgrowth of Paul's need to articulate his own experiences of channeling and psychic intuition, there seems to be an even more central concern. Paul told me of a sister-in-law whose body is riddled with cancer. His reactions to this situation were his most emotionally charged utterances during our three-hour conversation. "At a certain point," he announced, "technology fails us, and we have to go inward. The problem stimulates our ability to take control. We have to do something about it ourselves. Dealing with cancer requires the total resources of the total person. That's what we're all about at *Body, Mind & Spirit:* the whole person."

He continued in an animated, emphatic manner: "The point is that if I experience something, I know it. It's that inner, personal *knowing* that is most valuable. If a psychic or a channel experiences it for me, I don't know it. The best psychics and channels in the world are available to us at *Body, Mind & Spirit,* and we don't use them to predict our own personal future or to solve our own problems. The message is: Don't give your power away."

Paul recalls that he started *Body, Mind & Spirit* (originally known as *Psychic Guide)* "as a hobby" while he was pursuing a career in advertising. In the early days of his new publishing venture, Paul wrote almost its entire contents, resorting to a variety of pseudonyms to conceal the fact. He gave me a copy of the first issue, indicating that he is not proud of it. BMS's "real circulation" has grown to nearly 170,000. "We have been successful," he maintains, "because awareness is changing. Thank you, Shirley MacLaine. Thank you, Mrs. Reagan." (Nancy Reagan's alleged reliance on a California astrologer had been made public a few weeks earlier.) "We're not threatening," he added. "You don't have to leave your church or join ours. We don't criticize anyone—not even those who criticize us. We say, 'Just accept where you are. You put yourself there.' "

Our conversation turned to the question of the New Age concept of evil. "Is anything absolutely right or absolutely wrong?" I asked. Paul's response: "We've created this place for learning. It has rules. You've got to understand it in order to change it." Several stories told by Paul had the same message: There is an order to the universe, an order that is disclosed to "the explorer" through spiritual/psychic experiences. This order is moral. For example, he talked about a celebrated psychic who predicted commodities futures. "For a while, he was successful," Paul claimed. "But after a few weeks, his forecasts were wrong. You can't use your gifts for selfish gain." Then he appealed to the mystery at the center of his understanding of the New Age (and of life): "There is a certain way the universe works, and science has not been able to tell us what it is. Have fun with it. Don't be serious."

Two anecdotes from our rambling dialogue have stuck with me. They seem to encapsulate Paul. The day before our visit, he was in a grocery store with one of his children. He stopped at a display of canned pineapple juice. For some reason, it held his interest. He picked up a can and rubbed his fingers over it. Then he put it down and left the store without buying any pineapple juice. When he got home, he found that his brother and brother's family had arrived for an unexpected visit. His brother had brought a gift—a bottle of Southern Comfort, which Paul loves to drink with pineapple juice. Because he had neglected the strong urging in the store, he had to do without it. According to Paul, "There is a message to me in this. I should trust my inclinations." I mentioned that my positive hunches are not necessarily right but that, in my experience, my negative ones usually are. He disagreed.

He also told me about a ghost that haunted his house and was particularly bothersome to one of his children. He asked a close friend who is a medium what to do. His friend taught him how to summon the spirit so that he could ask it to leave his house—which it did. "But I wonder," he indicated, "if what I did really worked."

And so Paul remains open to all possibilities, but suspicious of all claims. "In all the time I've studied these things," he commented, "I've encountered only one or two truly paranormal events." He believes in channeling, has been a channeler himself, but is bored by the predictability and superficiality of most channeled messages. "Even if the channels are in touch with the dead, a departed spirit only knows what it did when it was alive." Why then, he muses, should we give up our power and allow our lives to be governed by such entities? Yet he salts his conversations with post-mortem quotations from Mark Twain and John Lennon, which have been communicated to him by channelers. Likewise he thinks that there are genuine gurus, but he is convinced that the content of most of the books written by the more prolific gurus could be reduced to one or two pages. He is disturbed by the I-have-all-the-answers attitude of the gurus, but he accepts their advertising in his magazine. "We have to eat, too," he states in his nonchalant, matter-of-fact manner. Then the other shoe drops: "But we are getting more selective."

CHAPTER FOUR

A Man for "All Seasons"

Unhappy women are given to protecting their sensitiveness by cynical gossip, by whining, by high-church and new-thought religions, or by a fog of vagueness.

—Sinclair Lewis, *Main Street*

New Age has few formal places of worship. Its rituals rarely depend on clergy, priests, or other holy personages. New Age is a network of people, books, periodicals, clichés, conferences, psychic faires, and inchoate feelings. At the center of the New Age life-style is the occult bookstore. Here ideas are disseminated, music is played, incense is wafted, authors and gurus attain star status, newspapers and periodicals are distributed, and conferences and workshops are advertised. In this low-key atmosphere, the knowing—the store owners and clerks—initiate the unknowing ("You're looking for a good book on crystal healing? Well, this is our best seller, but it's not nearly as good as that one over there. No. Not the red book. The sort of rose-colored one, right next to the geodes." "You're looking for a new color therapist? Have you heard about John _____ ? He comes in here all the time.")

At times when I am researching a project, I like to find a comfortable, convivial place and just hang out, listening to the interaction, observing what people say and what they buy.

There is a place I shall call "All Seasons," an occult bookstore in a college town that is such a genial place. The owners and the clerks know me and that I am interested in New Age phenomena. So they are tolerant of my sitting around for a few hours, perusing the books, engaging them and their customers in conversation, or just crouching silently in a corner, involved in people-watching. Some authors hang around bars, others frequent police stations. I prefer bookstores.

No two occult bookstores are alike. Each has its own personality (and personalities), its own colors, its own sounds, and its own fragrances. Occult bookstores are much more different from one another than, say, one Bible bookstore is from another. Some occult bookstores are ugly hole-in-the-wall places, specializing in astrology, numerology and selling rocks by the gram. Others have resident fortune-tellers. Some offer whatever the public wants; others refuse to sell books that advocate drug use or gay life-styles or anything that turns the owner off. Some bookstores have bulletin boards crammed with meeting notices and the business cards of local practitioners of various New Age arts. Others make no referrals or call attention only to the particular guru whose followers own the store.

Speaking of gurus—are you looking for one? Will a channeler or a yoga instructor do? Need a new macrobiotic diet? Want to take a course in astral projection? Seeking a Sufi dance? Hoping to meet a compatible Gemini? Have you seen your aura lately? Ready for rebirthing? Would a massage help? Have you fire-walked yet? New Age bookstores, together with health food stores, are the main distribution points for the magazines, newspapers, yellow page directories, and catalogs of services and practitioners. Without a doubt, these publications are the thread that stitches together the fabric of the Age of Aquarius.

The customers who frequent one store may be nothing like the customers at the next. All Seasons' clients have a particular look and feel. They are almost all women in their thirties. They look wan and listless. They barely speak above a whisper. Many of them have racially mixed children. The husbands or lovers of most have long since abandoned them. The women are sweet, nonassertive, and physically weak. My friend Emma, who is a clerk at All Seasons, thinks the colorless, sickly look is a manifestation of macrobiotic dieting. She also tells me that half of the store's clientele is gay/lesbian and that most of the women have been abused by parents or parent surrogates as children and repeatedly by spouses or lovers as adults.

While I continued my people-watching one day, a small, brown-haired woman brought a quartz crystal to the counter and paid for it in cash. She walked a few steps toward the door, stopped, slowly turned, walked back to the register, and in a virtually inaudible voice asked Emma the clerk: "How do I charge this?" Emma, who is notorious for her sense of humor, replied, "With your Visa or Mastercard!" Not getting the joke, the woman looked confused. Impetuously, I tried to help. "Here, let me do it for you," I offered. The woman handed me the crystal. I stroked it several times, held it to the light, stroked it again, and returned it to her. "That should do," I commented. A shy smile and a softly spoken "thank you" were my reward.

When the woman had left, Emma challenged me: "Ah, so you do believe in crystals after all. You told me that you did not." I don't, but "charging" the crystal seemed the thing to do at the time, so I charged it.

"Mandy," another clerk, approached me. She is a large, friendly brunette, who works as a volunteer at a nearby New Age center—the kind of place where famous authors and gurus give weekend workshops before moving on to the next center and the next, and where local talent fills in with weeknight sessions on the full gamut of New Age topics, from deepening one's relationships through massage to grieving for a deceased pet. She tried to engage me in conversation. "You know what I like about New Age?" she asked rhetorically. "It's that there are no absolutes—everything is relative."

Feeling a bit devilish, I responded: "Including what you just said? Is that relative, too?"

She looked stunned. "I don't know what you mean," she protested.

"Well," I replied, "you just uttered an absolute statement. You said that everything is relative. Is that statement relative as well?" I tried to explain my point to Mandy and to a few of the clerks and customers who joined the conversation. My argument: I doubt that New Age is as fully relativistic as its adherents think. I detect many implicit and explicit absolutes, and I wish that New Agers would examine and systematize what they believe.

Somehow the conversation turned to reincarnation. "After all, who is to say that we are right?" Mandy asked. "Hindus and Buddhists have believed in reincarnation for thousands of years."

"I wonder," I countered, "if what they believe has anything to do with your idea of reincarnation. Reincarnation presupposes that the *personality* is reborn—with its memories slightly dimmed but otherwise intact. Yet, Eastern religions, as I understand them, would argue that anything that one might remember is a manifestation of the finite, temporal existence. When this person dies [I pointed to myself], everything about it that is unreal, which includes my memories, my desires, my efforts, dies with it. That which is reborn is the true self, the manifestation of the divine within me. So how can the next manifestation recall this life?"

A customer chimed in that her aunt, through regressive hypnosis, had "remembered" that she was Cleopatra in a previous life. "Why Cleopatra?" I demanded. "Why do so many people believe they were Cleopatra? Why not Sam the fish peddler?" A clerk asked me if I had read a book by Dr. So-and-so, which explained that if one had been a member of

Cleopatra's court in a previous life, one could become confused by the memories of court life and come to the mistaken conclusion that one had been Cleopatra. The explanation failed to move me. I still wondered why people tend to remember that they were richer, more powerful, more interesting, and sexier in their previous lives than they are now.

Another customer broke in with: "The point is that each of us makes his or her own reality."

"What does that mean?" I asked. "Can you make it rain?"

Once again, everyone looked confused. Emma, who loves to clarify the obscure and obfuscate the clear, jumped in with a story about a customer who had just left when I came in. "She really got me upset," Emma declared. "She believes that whatever happens to people in this life they have decided to make happen before they were born. Do you know what she said when I asked her about the millions of Jews that were murdered by the Nazis? She said that they chose to be murdered so that they could learn a lesson from it—so that they could be better in their next lives. I almost went over the counter after her. I wanted to wring her neck!"

"Yes, but you have forgotten what she told you," blurted Mandy. "There is no such thing as murder because the murderer and the victim are one."

"Then why do we lock up and execute murderers?" I wanted to ask, but I felt I was being too combative and did not want to become *persona non grata* in my favorite New Age hangout. The afternoon continued. Emma introduced me to several customers: "This is Lowell. He knows everything about gurus and cults. Just ask him!" And I fielded hundreds of question about Da Free John, Sun Myung Moon, Sri Chinmoy, Guru Maharaj Ji, Elizabeth Claire Prophet, L. Ron Hubbard, and others. Now and then, the conversation would stray to *The Book of Miracles*, a channeled classic, purported to be messages from Jesus, which is studied in classes throughout the world. Emma would ask me to keep my voice

down since my remarks might offend a significant percent-
age of the All Seasons clientele.

   At seven o'clock the store closed. Emma, my wife, and I
went to dinner at a nearby Chinese restaurant. While we were
there, it rained and stormed and thundered and lightninged
as though it were time to build an ark. When the storm was
directly overhead and the lightning flashes came to earth
only yards away, Emma clung with one hand to the crystal she
wore around her neck and, shaking a fist in my face, cursed
me for challenging her friends to make it rain. "Whenever
someone does that," she sputtered, "it always pours!"

CHAPTER FIVE

Stories

Enough

The tale is told of a village in eastern Europe. The village was endangered. The townspeople sought the help of their rabbi, who was famous for his piety and wisdom. The rabbi went to a special place in the woods. There he built a special fire and offered a special prayer. It was enough. The village was spared.

Generations passed, and the village was once again in danger. The townspeople went to the grandson of the great rabbi and sought his aid. He went to the special place in the woods. He had forgotten the special way to build the fire, but he remembered the special prayer. It was enough. The village was spared.

Generations later, the village was again endangered. The great-great-grandson of the great rabbi went to the special place in the woods. But he did not know how to build the special fire, and he had forgotten the prayer. But it was enough, and the village was spared.

Many, many years later the village was imperiled. The great-great-great-great-grandson of the great rabbi went into the woods. But he could not locate the special place or build the special fire or offer the special prayer. So he told the story. And it was enough.

Shifting Paradigms and Telling Stories

As we have seen, proponents of the New Age appeal to their sense of a "paradigm shift," an alteration in values and attitudes. For them, the old age is moribund and worthless;

the new is revolutionary and irresistible. Many Christian thinkers and activists represent a similar demand for a societal shift in consciousness, a kind of corporate *metanoia* or repentance. Whether or not they use the term, for them New Age is an insistent, yet imprecise, demand, a categorical imperative, a striving after that which constantly eludes our grasp. I find this sense of New Age implicit in my friend John Snow's book *The Impossible Vocation: Ministry in the Mean Time*. Snow, professor of pastoral theology at the Episcopal Divinity School in Cambridge, Massachusetts, was born in 1924. He recalls the standards by which his parents' generation lived:

> The middle-class values of this society were prudence, patience, fiscal honesty, sexual constancy in marriage, lifelong marriage, hard work, keeping promises, modesty, telling the truth, patriotism, loyalty to friends, cheerfulness . . . responsibility of all adults for all children, a "good" education, sobriety . . . and democracy (treating tradespeople and servants with respect).

He fondly remembers the stability of his first eighteen years: "We had the same mailman, neighborhood policeman, grocer, druggist, pediatrician, family doctor, school teachers, Episcopal minister, Roman Catholic monsignor, plumber, electrician, and garage mechanic."[1]

Here was a world whose order was dependable and secure. Here was a moral universe "mightily buttressed by the absence of reliable birth control or safe abortion, the absence of transiency in the neighborhood, and the mutual assessment of character that went with this stability."[2]

What have we lost? What has changed? Snow inquires. Clearly we have already undergone a *paradigm shift*. We no longer look at the world or at our place in it as we once did. We have declared the old morality stifling, but we have found nothing better to hold our marriages, our families, our communities, or our inner selves together. We have adopted a "dog eat dog," "survival of the fittest" Darwinism; praised winners and pitied losers; prayed that God would reward our efforts as individuals with success; and hedged our prayers with the purchase of an occasional lottery ticket.

Competition has replaced cooperation; the issue of what works has ousted concern about what is right. Our religions provide us not with membership in exemplary communities or visions of a better world or surrogate families, but rather with "peace of mind" so that we can exploit and be exploited with as little stress as possible. As Snow notes: "A great many people in the United States . . . sense that there is something wrong; the old ways are passing without any trustworthy new ways to take their place."[3]

In the voices of ordinary people, Snow discerns "a sense of fear, aggravated by the unpredictability and general untrustworthiness of our corporate life."[4] Our economy, our judicial, educational, public health and ecological systems, our sexuality, are experienced as submerged in problems for which there seem to be no solutions, issues for which there are "no trustworthy moral guidelines, no moral criteria to help us live through them with hope and with some assurance that we are good people, not merely lucky or unlucky, winners or losers."[5]

We can attempt to rectify the moral slipperiness of today by lionizing the family values and ethical assumptions of an earlier time. But not even nostalgia is what it used to be! As new authors, film-makers, and playwrights come along, their images of the way it used to be are not derived from the Norman Rockwell small town America of the 1920s or the heroic years of struggle during the Great Depression and World War II. "The way it used to be" that is fondly remembered is the era of Elvis, James Dean, Marilyn Monroe, JFK, hula hoops, and large-finned sedans. And since the 1950s and 1960s got us into the present morass of morale and morality, who would want to return to such less than halcyon days?

One paradigm shift got us into the present mess. Can

another save us? The point is that we really do not have a choice. As Cass Elliott of the Mamas and the Papas once sang: "There's a new day coming." More than a century earlier, black slaves proclaimed the same sentiment as they awaited the Day of Jubilee. When one set of assumptions about family, career, nature, responsibilities, and God are no longer thought to work, another set (or other sets) will not be long in coming.

Living in the "mean time," in a time that is both *in between* and *nasty*, in a continual state of transition, is painful. But where there is hope—in a vision of a better world or a coming kingdom or liberation from enslavement or the building of community—it is also exciting and empowering. Ultimately that is what New Age is all about—seeing what ought to be and committing oneself to bringing it into existence. New Age is the consciousness of visionaries, of dreamers, and of poets. But more than this, it is what transpires when ordinary people allow the extraordinary to break into their lives, when they are unable to avoid living in the gap between what is and what can be.

During such a time, it is not beliefs, traditions, and certainties that impel or nourish. It is the shared story, the anecdote, the metaphor. As in Chaucer's *Canterbury Tales*, the personal stories of the pilgrims are of greater significance to us than are their road maps. When men and women live in continual, mysterious encounter with the Real, what is important to us as human and humane beings is revealed (as well as concealed) by the narratives of pilgrims. Narratives, of course, suffer a double disadvantage. They are filtered through both the personality of the storyteller and the consciousness of the hearer. In a sense, they prove everything and nothing.

When dealing with controversial issues, Snow recommends the method favored by some Native American councils of having each member "speak his piece" without interruption, comment, or criticism. He reports a discussion of homosexuality by a group of Christians that followed this format. He explains: "Each person present took enough time to tell how they had learned about homosexuality, what they were told about it, how they first encountered it in another person, how their ideas from their first knowledge of and encounter with homosexuality shaped their later understanding of it."[6] In such discussions without blame, judgment or debate, a space is opened up for persons to hear one another, to discover commonalities, to see the origins of the differences that divide. Even if not an inkling of consensus arises in the process, an opportunity is occasioned to discover that what is held in common is more important than that which divides.

Instead of debating an issue until someone wins and someone loses, the non-adversarial method enables each participant to hear the others and to know that he or she has also been heard. Snow feels that such a method is helpful in building a moral consensus. Whether or not he is right, it allows the stories to be told. And, often, that is enough.

Frequently when I am told stories by my New Age friends, I catch myself about to say, "I wonder. . . ." Having been a very close observer of chicanery and nonsense for so many years, my first impulse is to want to explain my friends' stories away, to grind them up with categories and catch phrases from my research. But when the desire to hear the story and discover the meaning that my friends have created for themselves dominates, I restrain my "Yes, but—" and "I have seen it all and know better" responses and simply listen. "I wonder," as in "I have mental reservations" gives way to an empathetic sharing of my friends' wonder and awe. Then, because my friends want me to, I tell my own stories—a few of which follow.

Daydreaming

When there are forty-plus students and one teacher, the chances of one-to-one interaction are remote. A very bright

pupil might bask for a minute every now and then in the
warmth of a teacher's praise. A "bad boy" could attract a
reprimand a day. A class clown could fare likewise. But a just
better than average scholar, lost in the back seats of the far
row, was neither seen nor heard, neither honored nor
reproved by his teacher. Since the workbook assignments and
the tedious blackboard explanation of reading, writing, and
arithmetic required little time or attention, other means had
to be found to consume the hours until the three o'clock bell
signaled the end of the day.

The only sure salvation from tedium was daydreaming.
Hidden behind my passive demeanor, I was fighting wars,
flying overhead, rounding up stampeded cattle, inflicting
pain on playground bullies, and tying little girls' pigtails to
their chairs. Sometimes the daydreaming would deepen into
an altered state of conscious, whose connection to wakeful-
ness was tenuous.

And sometimes when I daydreamed, I found that I could
"remember" the future. I could predict with certainty who
would be called on by the teacher, who would be sick
tomorrow, and the exact amount that would be donated by
my class to the Junior Red Cross. Such memories in advance
were trivial. If I tried, I could catch glimpses of things yet to
be—but since I was only a child, I had no idea of what they
meant or how to communicate what I saw to anyone else.

As a child, I looked ahead to men on the moon—but
thought that they communicated with the earth by telepathy.
I knew that two of my classmates would not live to adulthood,
saw another in prison, and another dying in his twenties
when a streetcar and a gasoline truck collided.

I would start crying suddenly with the realization that
Grandmother Streiker would soon die. But as hard as I might
try to see their fate, I could conjure up no picture of Gramma
or Grampa Peller. Perhaps they would live forever.

Knowing the future was like remembering the past—it was
capricious and creative. The images were murky and partial;

they came and went as they pleased, not as I desired; they were in no particular order, and they overlapped. Most of the time, I could not interpret what they were until after they actually came to pass. I decided that this was a gift that I did not want—only to receive a new one. Other minds began to communicate with mine. Gramma Peller's would tell me of her loneliness and ask me to visit. Unknown voices would crowd in. I did not know who or where they were, but I was assailed by their greetings, exhortations, and opinions as unavoidably as though I sat in a room filled with shouting cohorts. One of these beings told me that he was a Martian. But why should I believe him or even think that his voice came from a place other than my imagination?

I started to see the picture of the blue-eyed one who would be the great love of my life and who would love me as I so fervently wanted to be loved.

And I began to hear the voice of God, began to feel attracted by an overwhelming acceptance and, at the same time, cast away by an energy too intense for me to cope with. God was always there, like the air and the sunlight—a presence as unavoidable as having to go to school. From time to time, Jesus would come down from the altar cross of our neighborhood Catholic church, Our Lady of Angels, and beckon to me.

Sometimes I thought that I was very special. Sometimes I was afraid that I was going crazy.

But the best daydreaming of all had no content. It was like being half asleep though fully alert at the same time, resting on the bosom of the universe, feeling sound, secure, and at peace—feeling as though there were no boundaries or limitations, as though I were everywhere in the universe at once and the whole universe were fully present in me. I would lull myself into such states by imagining that I was sitting in a row boat on Lake Michigan, staring at the waves, rocking gently in the breeze. Suddenly my body would be left behind in the boat, and I would soar throughout the galaxy as the galaxy cavorted within me—until the voice of doom would abruptly seize hold of my consciousness and pull me back to earth with those horrible words: "Lowell Streiker! Are you paying attention?"

Intimations of Eternity

Mirrors mirrored by mirrors. Reflections of reflections of reflections. The barbershop around the corner from my father's office had a child's chair, carved to resemble a carousel horse. When I was deemed too big for it, I was moved to an adult chair. A special seat was placed between the handles of the barber's chair to bring my head to the proper height. After the barber cut my hair, he showed me the back of my head by pointing to the mirror in front of me and holding a large, rectangular hand mirror behind my back. When the mirrors were aligned just so, an infinity trap was produced—an endless reflection of reflections would sweep me into a state of wonder, which would hold me spellbound until the barber set down his hand mirror.

Comic books often used a variant of the infinity trap. On the cover, the hero would be depicted holding a comic book on which he was depicted holding a comic book on whose cover he stood holding a comic book. . . .

Pigeons circling overhead at Garfield Park on a warm afternoon often sent me into a trance. As long as I watched them for an hour or so, their cries and the flapping of their wings and the gentle lapping of the lagoon waters would grow silent. Time stood still, and I was at one with the world. He who gaped at the bird-filled sky and the bird-filled sky at which he gaped were one.

A family visit to a cemetery to pay our respects to my father's father, his sister, and relatives whom I had never known was another infinity trap. I would wander among the tombstones, reading of long-dead parents, brothers, sisters, and children, imagining the tragedies that had brought death to the young, the relief felt by those who had lived too long, and sorrow of those left behind. Suddenly it would all swirl together. The dead would stand silent and surround me, uttering not a word, showing not a trace of emotion. I would run to the lilac bushes and tear off sprigs as souvenirs of my silent communion with the dead and as evidence that I was alive. This act became my ritual to bring me back to the land of the living and to secure me there until my next cemetery visit.

My grandmother would show me her unsorted and unmounted collection of photographs—images of World War II mixed in with pictures of adults in Victorian garb, boys wearing knickers and caps, girls in woolly chaps on the photographer's pony. After an hour or so, I would become lost in time, not knowing whether I were in the photographs looking out at the present or in the present staring at images of the past. An afternoon with an elderly relative, someone distant with whom I had not previously spent time, could produce the same effect. Suddenly I was not a child listening to what it was like when Great-aunt Clara or Great-uncle Phil was a child. I was an immigrant in steerage, catching my first glimpse of the New World and wondering how much wealth I could pluck from the streets of gold.

Parades were special to me. Throughout the war years, the bands and the older veterans marched down Washington Boulevard in Maywood, Illinois. Much sooner than I desired, the parade would peter out, some disarrayed Cub Scout troop bringing up the rear. But a part of me would witness an endless parade—a march of the living and the dead. I could see and hear and feel the infinite parade as the honor guards, drill teams, drum and bugle corps, marching bands, and civic groups marched by. The reality of my private parade would linger for a few minutes after the crowd dispersed and the last beat of the bass drums faded into silence. "Left, left, left, right, left," some unseen drill sergeant would call out, and something inside me would have no choice but to march.

Then the feeling of endless marching would ebb away like the glow of the tiny ember of an extinguished wooden match. But it would never be completely gone. (Even as I watched the festive parades, my grandparents' neighbors' children were marching to their death from Bataan. We would learn this years later.)

The animals at the Brookfield and Lincoln Park zoos winked at me and whispered about eternity. The scary crocodiles and menacing pythons could swallow a child whole. Yet, within the terror was a strange peace—a sense of propriety, proportion, and justice.

The mirrors, the pigeons, the comic book covers, the cemeteries, the photos from yesterdays, the distant relatives, the parades, the predators and I were one and the same, a hand of playing cards spread on a table, fanning out forever, intimations of eternity.

The Lure

I cannot remember a time when I did not feel the lure, did not sense that I was being drawn toward something profound and indescribable. No matter what I might be engaged in, I was distracted by a sense that something was missing, something without which I could never be satisfied or fulfilled. I remember watching those old musical comedies in which the ingenue (Jane Powell or Judy Garland) asked her father or uncle or guardian (S. K. "Cuddles" Sakall or Lauritz Melchior) how she would know when she was in love. "Don't worry. When the time comes, you'll just know," the wise old one would intone. And eventually, after the requisite false starts, deceptions, misunderstandings, and red herrings, true love would gush out in exaggerated feelings and appropriate ballads, accompanied by an invisible 100-piece orchestra. And I knew, as I sat in the darkness on those Saturday afternoons at the Alamo theater, stuffing myself with popcorn and Mason Dots, that the movies were telling the truth. True love was out there somewhere—an object of devotion that would sweep me away and an acceptance that would never let me go. There was something that would overwhelm my senses and capture my heart. And it would all happen in technicolor to the accompaniment of violins, cymbals, and drums!

Similar feelings would flood my being when I gazed out on Lake Michigan or when I strolled the city parks in spring or wandered Thatcher Woods in autumn. The reflections of light on the water, the shimmering iridescence of green grass and leaves, the flaming displays of the forest in September moved me so deeply that it hurt.

Sometimes I just surrendered to whatever it is that undergirds all things. I would relax and drift in a state of reverie, half awake and half asleep, and feel as secure as when I lay with my head in Gramma Peller's lap. In this state, I could daydream, fantasize, write as though some other being had taken possession of my hand and was writing through me.

And there was the ever-present companion. Someone walked alongside me. Someone cared. There was a presence I could address and who would respond. This someone was more than the "imaginary playmate" whom the young child blames for his own misdeeds. From the ages of ten to fifteen, I could hear his voice and know with assurance that he heard mine. But who was he?

He told me he was "Lars from Mars" or "Lars Martian." There was a comic book titled *Lars of Mars*, which existed for two issues in 1951, when I was twelve. I don't think I ever saw it. Perhaps I did, and the name lodged in my brain. He told me little of Mars or of himself. He was a companion who listened to my problems, helped me sort out the possible solutions, and supported my decisions. He was a kind of invisible counselor, a monitor who constructively criticized my development and approved of who I was.

Now and then, I would tell a chum or playmate about Lars,

only to be derided. I even mentioned Lars to my parents one night when "Uncle" Roy and "Aunt" Pat were visiting. They seemed embarrassed and quickly changed the subject.

When I was a high school sophomore of fifteen, I attended a meeting of the Chicago Rocket Society with other members of the Science Club. The speaker was a well known UFO contactee, who claimed to have been taken up into a flying saucer by its Venusian flight crew. The only UFOs I had seen were in Hollywood films like *The War of the Worlds* and *The Day the World Stood Still*, and I had read reports in the Chicago newspapers. The audience consisted mostly of technically inclined types who dismissed the contactee as a humbug. But the adolescents from the Science Club were deeply impressed. As we sat together at the back of the room, I told them about my years of communication with Lars. One of them, a senior named Ted gave an excited account of a book he had read about "Project Bluebook," a government inquiry into UFOs. Another student began waving a book he had been reading, pointing to photographs of "spacecraft." Simultaneously, yet another teenager was babbling about documented instances of mental telepathy and of a time in the future when psychic communication would replace radio and the telephone.

Flying saucers, creatures from outer space, an invisible Martian who communicated by means of telepathy—it all seemed to fit together and possess credibility, at least to me and many of my peers. Hearing the violins, cymbals, and drums, I dashed to the nearest phone booth and called the girl I was then dating to tell her of this suddenly coherent world I had somehow entered. As we spoke, Tony, a short, olive-complexioned classmate (whom the contactee had singled out as bearing an uncanny resemblance to a Venusian space traveler he had met on the UFO), ran to the phone booth and began tugging at the door handle. "I have to tell you," he yelled, "I just heard a voice saying, 'Lowell is telling the truth. Listen to what he says.' "

I lost my inhibitions about Lars. I became a minor celebrity—classmates wanted to hear my story, wanted me to hear theirs, gave me books (ranging from science fantasy to alleged scientific accounts of the lost civilizations of Atlantis and Mu), and arranged for me to speak before small gatherings that they arranged at their homes. When I was alone, I would ask Lars questions, and all the way from his home on Mars he would answer, giving me new material to present at the next impromptu meeting of my friends. An elderly English teacher encouraged my interest. She invited me to speak to her classes. She was a Unitarian, but was finding little comfort in her religion as her life ebbed. She was sure that telepathic communication with Martians somehow promised immortality to earthlings.

"You're making a laughingstock of yourself and of us," my mother warned. Not everyone who listened to my tales was sympathetic. Some made fun of me; some thought I was crazy. But it was all exciting, and involving. I felt special, the center of attention, and REAL. That much of the attention was negative made no difference. Attention is attention is reality.

"A Figment of the Imagination"

When I became a Christian at the age of fifteen, Lars became a problem. What was the difference between listening to the voice of God and conversing with Lars, my constant companion?

A week after my conversion, I met a cute, tiny blonde from Park Ridge at a journalism conference held at my mother's alma mater, Proviso High School in Maywood. Sharon and I were seated side by side, and at precisely the same moment, we turned to each other and began to witness—I with my copy of the tract "Four Things God Wants You to Know," and she with her pocket New Testament. She was also a brand-new Christian.

I found her attractive and wished that we could start

dating, but her parents made it clear that they did not approve of a Jew from the city. Worse than that, I reminded them of the "lipstick killer," who had left "please catch me before I kill again" scribblings on the bodies of his victims—one of whom was buried a short distance from Sharon's home. Moreover, she was already going steady with a boy from her high school—the very kid I had handily defeated for the position of Auditor of Public Accounts at Boys' State the previous summer. But now and then, we found time for each other. She would take the Greyhound bus into the Loop, and we would spend the day together— walking, shopping, going to the Art Institute.

Although we were about the same age, she drew interest from the capital amassed by her older brother, a college student active in Inter-Varsity Christian Fellowship. I remember how deeply she embarrassed me by telling me that her brother, who was married, had informed her that "sex is a tonic to the system." At age fifteen, never having kissed a girl except while playing post office at my cousin Charlotte's birthday party, the thought of having intercourse appealed to me about as much as the prospect of jumping out of an airplane without a parachute.

As Sharon and I shared accounts of our respective conversions and spiritual growth, I told her about my longtime association with a Martian—with whom, of course, I often discussed theology. Lars had told me that God had incarnated himself in a Martian form and had died for the sins of Martians as well—which seemed fair to me.

Sharon was horrified; she abruptly changed the subject. There were now two taboos (sex and Mars), two parents, anti-semitism, a mass murderer, and a steady boyfriend standing between us. Things were not promising.

We continued to correspond and to see each other in the city. During our next visit, she assaulted me with the news from her brother-the-theologian that Lars was a demon who was trying to subvert my faith and that I should abruptly cease our communications.

I was fond of Sharon and still hoped that a kissing-and-hugging, but certainly not a tonic-for-the-system, relationship might develop. Further, I respected her theologically adept brother. So I stopped receiving or sending between earth and other planets—for good.

The subject of my communication with Lars came up again about a year later. My parents, unwilling to accept my conversion, and assuming that some underlying pathology was controlling my behavior, took me to a prominent child psychiatrist, whom I shall call Samuel Kleinfeld. Kleinfeld was, at first, quite hostile toward my Christian faith, accusing me of having converted only to get even with my mother for her occasional punitive outbursts. According to Kleinfeld, my sense of communion with a supernatural being was an infantile projection. I, of course, disagreed. Kleinfeld insisted that there was no difference between letting Jesus into my heart or being led by the Spirit and my association with Lars Martian. I protested that Lars had been "a figment of my imagination," but that God was real.

After exhaustive psychological tests revealed to Dr. Kleinfeld that my motives were neither anger nor hostility (the psychologist who tested me said that I was "the most Christlike person he had ever encountered"), he apologized to me, explaining that he had allowed his anti-Christian feelings (the result of his persecution by the Nazis) to influence his professional evaluation. He remained concerned about the extremity of my convictions and the over zealousness of my witnessing, Bible study, and so on. He stated: "You have all your eggs in one basket. And if that basket breaks, you will need help. I will be here if you decide you need that help." Kleinfeld felt that my interpretation of one particular Rorschach ink blot was significant. I had seen a cross with a cloud over it. No doubt, Kleinfeld pontificated, this meant underlying doubts as to my Christian faith.

Sharon had convinced me that Christians would not tolerate my ongoing conversations with extra-terrestrial beings. Dr. Kleinfeld had forced me to declare that Lars was a delusion. Once I had uttered the words *figment of my imagination*, there was no going back. Saying it had made it so.

I suppose today I would tell Dr. Kleinfeld that every thought one has, every attitude, every value is colored by one's imagination, interpreted by one's imagination, and cloaked and distorted by one's imagination. In the process of living, we try out our perceptions, make adjustments, and grow. Lars had been more real to me than Samuel Kleinfeld. The myths that give meaning to our lives are more real than anything else can be. And one is legitimately sad when any myth may no longer be entertained (nor any longer entertain).

The Late-Night Visitor

I wake up from a deep sleep—not all at once, but ever so gradually. As I look at the foot of the bed, something seems to materialize. It looks like Misty, a friend of mine who is recovering from surgery at a hospital twenty miles from my home. But it looks more like a semi-transparent hologram, a special effect. I can look through her and see the furniture on the other side of the room. This wraith version of Misty glances at me and then at my wife, who is sound asleep next to me. Misty seems flustered. Her hand covers her mouth, and she vanishes.

Now fully awake, I slide my feet out of the bed and sit up. I notice that the illuminated digital clock face says "3:16." Dismissing it all as a vivid dream, I cuddle up with Connie and go back to sleep.

The next day when I visited Misty at the hospital, I was about to tell her about my "dream," when she interrupted me to relate an "out of the body" experience she had undergone the previous night. She said: "I woke up and wanted to talk to you. So I stood up and focused my energy. The next thing I knew I was standing at the foot of your bed, looking at you.

Then I saw Connie asleep next to you, and I realized that I should not be there. So I left."

I asked her whether she was wearing a plaid flannel shirt when this happened. She told me that she was. Then I asked her if she noticed the time of her "visit." She replied that she looked at her alarm clock when she went back to bed. It was 3:16 exactly. She said that she remembered it because it reminded her of a Bible verse from the Gospel of John that she had memorized in Sunday school when she was a child.

Shortly thereafter, Misty returned to her home in another state. With the exception of a postcard, I have never heard from her again.

During a business trip to England, I was entertained one afternoon at the home of Daphne Vane, one of the leaders of an anti-cult organization. I was telling her that many of my counseling cases have involved individuals whose lives were disrupted by their inability to deal with unusual "psychic" experiences. They felt that their unsought states of extra-sensory perception or precognition or astral projection were evidence either of their mental instability or of their "chosenness." Mrs. Vane added stories of her own about friends of hers.

Her husband thought that such tales were "rubbish," and he offered his common sense debunking of all his wife's stories, dismissing most as the hallucinations of overwrought individuals. I told him that I was not so sure. After all, I was a critical, skeptical observer of spiritual/psychic phenomena, and I myself had been visited by a convincing, three-dimensional, semi-transparent image of one of my friends.

"Nonsense," he insisted. "You were in love with her—that's all."

I wasn't, and I knew it. But how could I prove that to this empirically minded skeptic any more than I could demonstrate that the event I had reported had actually occurred? I've been told that when it comes to claims of spiritual and paranormal experiences, I'm an incredibly tough minded, hard sell. Yet, I know what I know. And John Vane is certainly no dummy. A few years after my visit to his home, he was awarded the Nobel prize for chemistry.

My wife's reaction to the late-night visitation: "Look, I don't care what your friends do during the daytime or where they send their astral bodies at night, just tell them that our bedroom is off limits!"

The Touch of Her Face

On a quiet Sunday afternoon, Connie and I were reading the newspaper in our bedroom. She dozed off, and I tried to rest my eyes by pretending to project myself to explore the hills and valleys of the rough-textured ceiling. In my drowsy state, I felt that I was actually wandering the white desert above me. Then I brought my astral self back. I turned and looked at Connie. I wondered what it would be like to inhabit her body. So I sent my astral self into her body. Then I marched her body as though it were my own into the bathroom and stared at her in the mirror, caressing her face. How soft and silky it felt from within her, much different when felt with her hands than with mine.

I returned her to our bed and retrieved my astral self from her. I was wide awake now, experiencing a sense of awe, love, and closeness to her as great as I have ever known. She slept on.

Dale

About ten years ago, my father-in-law died. He was going blind and did not want to be dependent on his loved ones, so he shot himself. I had only known him for a short time, and we had not been close. I had never really been comfortable with him, and he knew it. He was just too obtrusive and opinionated for me to deal with, so I sort of hid from him. He was a generous and loving man, whom I appreciated in many ways. But we just were not close.

I stepped in and handled the funeral arrangements for his widow as best I could. A few months later, Mom sold her home and came to live with us.

Along the way, a curious thing happened. I started to identify with Dale in ways that had not previously been possible. I drove his four-wheel-drive Bronco and fantasized about taking camping trips as he regularly had done—something that never interested me. I learned everything I could about his past from his friends and relatives, visited the town he had helped build in the Redding area, went through photo albums, and listened to his favorite country and western recordings. But the fantasies of becoming more like him were not very powerful. We were just too different.

Then one morning as I was walking our dogs, I looked up and saw him about a hundred yards ahead of me, wearing his usual windbreaker and walking with his familiar gait. One of the dogs distracted me for a second by pulling on his leash, and when I looked back, the man in the windbreaker was gone. I went to the spot where he had been and looked in every direction, but he was nowhere to be seen.

Was it Dale? Or just someone who, from a distance, resembled Dale? Could my guilt about never having gotten to know him or giving him the chance to know me have conjured up a hallucination or a mistaken identification? I will never know.

"The Heart Has Reasons. . . ."

Victor is a celebrated psychic. Many articles have been written about him. His friends include some of the most serious investigators in the field of psychic investigation. Numerous individuals bear witness to his abilities. I am not one of them.

As I was driving him to a social engagement one evening, I commented that in my opinion his interest in the "scientific" study of psi (psychic abilities) was inspired by his need to validate and justify his own experiences.

Victor flew into a rage, screaming that he had no need to prove his experiences to anyone. "It is clear to me," he shouted, "that you have never understood me." He was probably right. It was the end of our friendship.

Maybe Victor has some great psychic ability. There are parapsychologists who think so. But in the year that I knew him, I saw no evidence—witnessed no projections of his astral self, heard no predictions of the future, learned of no remote viewings, was provided with nothing but his own assertions of his remarkable abilities.

Perhaps if I had been part of his circle—if I had been trained in a formal program in parapsychology, had attended scholarly conferences and listened to papers about the study of psi, had friends with whom I could sit up into the wee hours of the morning comparing notes on my interests in psychic phenomena, it would have been different. "The heart has reasons reason knows not of." Psi is shy. It hides not only from skeptical inquirers who want to bring it into the laboratory under rigorous controls and examine it, but it also conceals itself from skeptics like me, who are willing to believe but are not in love with psi—that is, are not willing to accept uncritically and to suspend judgment. John Vane told me that I had seen because I had loved. Victor said, in effect, that I had not seen because I had not loved. And my experiences with Dale had proved to me that there is something in us that strives to conquer death itself by incorporating the loved one we have lost into our very being.

Young Soul, Old Soul

I remember a conversation of many years ago with my friend Abner, who was then a psychotherapist in Philadelphia. The subject was reincarnation—in which neither of us believed. Yet, we noticed in our own children certain tendencies of which transmigration was as good an explanation as any. We each had two children, one of whom was an "old soul" and one of whom was a "young soul." The "old souls" seemed to have an innate, intuitive understanding of human dynamics. Our respective "old soul" children were both second-born. There was rarely a need to teach them anything or to offer them correction; they already knew. They were comforting albeit a bit manipulative. An "old soul" could comfort a father when he was depressed, encourage him in his ventures, and provide remarkably sage advice— almost as soon as the child could talk. They could also get what they wanted by psychologically outmaneuvering us dads. "Young souls," on other hand, were naive and spontaneous. Everything had to be explained to them. A "young soul" could provide a father with hours of delight.

I have lost contact with Abner and his family, so I cannot describe how his children passed through childhood, adolescence, and entered into adulthood. As the father of my two children, I would say that whatever advantage the "older soul" held in early years slowly faded away. Today they are equal in intelligence and wisdom, although the curiosity and drive of the "younger soul" has led him to savor more new experiences (moving frequently from one part of the country to the next, pursuing active hobbies like skiing, flying, and hot-air ballooning). The "older soul" has excelled in quieter pursuits, such as earning college degrees and mastering the requirements of a demanding career.

Then there is the matter of the Renoir. One day at a supermarket, I stumbled upon an unframed print that was being sold as part of a promotion. It was a picture of my daughter, the "older soul." The face, the figure, the coloring, the hair, the shape of the model's hands were nearly identical with my daughter's. I went to the Barnes museum near Philadelphia, which has over one hundred Renoirs, hoping to see the original. But it was not there. As I wandered the aisles, I spotted a Modigliani—a portrait of my mother! My manuscript editor tells me: "I once found in an art gallery in Raleigh, North Carolina, a portrait of a woman who looked exactly like my younger cousin—but the painting was made over one hundred years ago!" What if . . . ?

How Remarkable Is Remarkable?

Everyone experiences remarkable coincidences. Just how remarkable do they have to be in order to require an explanation like "the hand of God" or "fate" or "the influence of planetary bodies"?

Years ago I was retained by a family to find their son, who was the member of a small sect. I learned that the group had left California and was living somewhere on the island of Hawaii. I discovered this through a friend of mine, who is also a counselor, one of whose clients had just defected from the group and had returned to the mainland. From her, we learned the approximate location of the group.

I decided that the best way to find the group was to track down the leader. According to my sources of information, she never left the group except when she went into town once a week to pick up supplies. Surely someone had spotted her in town or had seen her on the road. When the group had been located in Berkeley, they recruited members by attaching posters to lamp posts and telephone poles, inviting the public to meetings. The posters featured a large, clear photograph of the leader wearing a distinctive type of garb. I thought that by showing the photo to people in the community nearest to where the group was, I could discover exactly where they were. So I got on a jumbo jet for Hilo and was studying the picture when a woman wearing a costume like that of a nun walked past me and took a seat a few rows in front of mine. There was no mistake. It was the leader of the group!

When searching for another missing person in southern California, I ran into a stone wall. The young man had dropped out of college and was wandering around with a second man, distributing gospel tracts and preaching in public. I had no address or phone number. Further, my subject had not been seen in the area for weeks.

Through one of my police connections, I learned that the other young man had been arrested in Santa Barbara for urinating in public. But neither his whereabouts nor that of his partner was known.

I flew to Santa Barbara and tried to find his trail. I drove around aimlessly, hoping to run into some itinerant street preachers. I found a few, but they belonged to the sect known as the "Christ Family." While taking a break from the search, I visited a college professor of my acquaintance. I told him what had brought me to town. As we talked, a janitor swept the floor just outside my friend's office. The janitor interrupted us with an "excuse me." I assumed that he wanted to sweep the area where we were sitting. "Those fellows you're looking for," he blurted out, "I think they're staying in a house across from my apartment." They were.

God's Humor

There is a recurrent pattern of events in my life that I would describe as "doubling" or "God's jokes." If something unusual happens for the first time ever, it will probably happen again within a day. If I have never heard of a sect of vegetarian UFO contactees who live in a geodesic dome in downtown Burbank until someone calls me and asks for information, a second person will call the next day seeking the same data. If a family comes to see me because they are concerned about the group that I know only because of the first phone call asking for information, a second family will turn up on my doorstep the next day. If the first family is concerned about their daughter who is a left-handed, redheaded, Frisbee champion, the second family will have a daughter who is also a left-handed, redheaded, Frisbee champion.

If the author of a forthcoming book on computerized

fishing phones for background on a sect of Alaskan polygamous blubber merchants, the chances are that a second such author will be in touch before very long. And if I know absolutely nothing about such a group, the odds are high that first one and then another person will phone me with just the information I need.

There are probably rational explanations for these quirky surprises, but I have only one explanation for this phenomenon: "God has a sense of humor."

Psychic Parking Spaces

When Sande, a channeler, and I had concluded our first interview (described in the next chapter), my wife and I walked with her to the parking garage where she had left her car. Sande commented: "When I let Hera, my entity, drive, when I am conscious of her guidance, I always find parking spaces. When I forget and take control myself, I have trouble."

Sande's remark reminded me of two incidents. Several years ago, I was in Berkeley, California, with Al and Jeannie, a husband and wife, who were former members of the Peoples Temple. We were in their car on our way to a downtown restaurant. Legal parking spaces in Berkeley are virtually nonexistent. About a minute before we arrived at the front of the restaurant, Al turned to Jeannie and asked her "to materialize a parking space." It had begun to rain, so I was not in a mood to confront them with my skepticism. As we rounded the corner, a car left the parking spot right at the curb, a few feet from the door of the restaurant. Al turned to me and crowed, "She does that all the time!"

When I was a college student in Philadelphia, I supported myself and my family by preaching at a small Congregational church. I had no car and owned a single blue suit. Whenever I left our apartment in Germantown for the forty-five minute trolley ride and fifteen minute walk to the church, I would pray that God would prevent it from raining on me. For more than a year, there was not a drop of rain on Sundays or Wednesday nights. Then I began wondering about the tomato farmers in nearby New Jersey, who really needed the rain and were probably asking God for a steady downpour on Sundays and Wednesdays. How could God arrange for them to have rain and for me to be spared? A picture formed in my mind of the tri-state area divided into millions of separate patches of air space—one above each person. If all their prayers were answered at once, it would rain in some air spaces but not in others. What would meteorologists make of that?

Realizing that my prayers were self-centered and that my thinking was more magical than spiritual, I stopped addressing such petitions to God. For a long time, I stopped asking God altogether, and resolved to listen rather than to speak. For years, I was a mystic of the moment, content to respond to God as he addressed me in the midst of my life, as I found him luring me into fellowship with him. I became acutely aware of the numinous depths of everyday experience, of the opportunities to respond to God by unselfishly responding to other human beings. I saw God at work in the world of my most mundane experiences—heard him in the songs of Simon and Garfunkel and the Beatles, felt him calling a generation to transcend materialism and prejudice, but much more prosaically I sensed that the use of my talents and abilities on behalf of others expressed my partnership with the unseen ally. And how does one pray to a presence who is always there, always attendant, always responsive, and always demanding?

It took a great deal of pain to answer that question. In the depths of confusion and suffering, I found myself talking to God once more. The first prayers were little more than utterances, such as "Help!" But in time, I simply could not fail to pray, could not go through a day without conversing with my unseen ally. But still my spiritual life is overshadowed by the listening, by paying attention to the silences, by responding with the fullness of my being to the God who is present where I would never expect him to be if I gave it any thought. But I never ask for parking spaces.

Stuff Happens

When I was executive director of the Mental Health Association of Delaware, I was lobbying for the passage of an appropriations bill to improve mental health services. I walked into the Delaware House of Representatives and was stopped by a page, a woman in her twenties. "You know, it's really amazing," she whispered. "Cheryl, one of the other pages, said that while she was meditating she had a vision of a man who would come here this afternoon. She described him to me detail for detail, down to what he would be wearing. And you are that man." The awestruck young woman added: "You're probably not interested in this. It all sounds so crazy." I insisted that I was indeed interested and asked to meet Cheryl.

Cheryl did not seem the least bit surprised to see me. After all, she knew I was going to be there! She stated that she often had such precognitive flashes while meditating. I asked her what such things meant. "You mean," she answered rhetorically, "whether this means that if I have a vision of someone it means that we have unusual rapport or knew one another in a previous life or are destined to be lovers—something like that?" She then answered her own question: "Stuff happens. That's all the real meaning it has."

Transition

In the time between my years as executive director of mental health associations in Delaware and California and the present, more things happened than can be discussed here. For six years, I was director of Freedom Counseling Center, an agency that assisted families disturbed by the conversion of a loved one to cults and sects. In addition, the Center advised individuals whose lives had become confused as the result of unsettling psychic or spiritual experiences. The lessons of these years are found in my earlier books *Cults, Mind-Bending* and *The Gospel Time Bomb.*

My two thousand cases exposed me to more than one hundred different groups as well as numerous unusual personal experiences. My clients have included individuals who wanted to regain control of their lives from psychics, individuals who believed they were cursed by psychics, and individuals who considered themselves to be psychics. In addition, I have counseled persons who believed themselves to be demon-possessed, brainwashed, or under the mental domination of some group or person.

When I stumbled on so-called New Age phenomena, nothing seemed very new to me. But when I looked past the pathologies, the ripoffs, and the dependencies, I saw something familiar and almost comforting. As a counselor, I had become a kind of Better Business Bureau of Spiritual and Psychic Phenomena. I only heard the complaints and the bad news about religious experience. Along the way, as my own sense of spiritual identity grew, I wanted less and less to hear stories of the atrocities. I did not want to be party to a war against innovative and unusual experiences, groups, and geniuses. Yet, I wanted to retain my right to say "no thanks," to respect the viewpoints of others without sharing all experiences, blessing all groups, or accepting all geniuses as beneficent. I had passed from being an agent of gentle deconversion to being an avuncular friend. Somehow I had come to realize that even the worst fanatics are my brothers and sisters and that we are united in the prayer: "Thy kingdom come. Thy will be done."

Cups

When I was studying pentecostalism and the charismatic movement a few years ago, I discovered that private revelations had become big business. Several volumes of semipoetic musings have been published by various charismatics, purporting to be direct revelations ("words of wisdom or knowledge") from Jesus. Reading a few, I found that Jesus writes very badly these days. He has lost a lot of his bite and verve since the parables and the Sermon on the Mount. He has become a sickly sentimentalist, who combines pop-psych, advice to the lovelorn, and trite moral homilies.

While I was in a hair styling shop in Nashville, captive of a hairdresser with a razor in her hand, I agreed to allow her to read me her personal messages from Jesus, which she carried in a suitcase full of spiral-bound composition books. The first and most current message, which she recited from memory, was that "we are all cups—some of us full of blessings, some of us half-full and some of us empty. Why, some of us are cracked cups!" It was hard to take her seriously. Yet, I am sure that she was sincere and that her personal revelations were important to her and central to her life. She felt special, close to God, and comforted in what she described to me as her lonely existence. One of her books of messages from Jesus presented "the true spiritual meaning of Walt Disney's *Bambi.*" According to her account, Jesus explained that Bambi is the Christian soul seeking spiritual maturity; the fire is lust, which would destroy us if it could; Thumper is the true church.

I wonder who is really communicating Jesus's latest messages: the charismatics or the channelers?

Linda

I have a friend, Linda, with whom I attended high school. Today she lives in a large city in the South. When I first knew her, she was a fundamentalist Christian. Years later, she became a charismatic. Now she is a channeler and a crystal healer. However, she claims that she is still a born-again Christian who speaks in tongues and has the gift of healing. Her New Age skills simply add to who she is as a spiritual human being. Nothing is subtracted.

For me, fundamentalism, pentecostalism, and New Age are three competing, logically incompatible mythic structures—three different ways of relating oneself meaningfully to the universe and relating the universe meaningfully to one's life. I can see the overlap between fundamentalism and pentecostalism. Each is based on common assumptions about Jesus, the Bible, salvation, the Second Coming, and so on. Yet, they diverge on the subject of "gifts of the Spirit," and eventually each is intolerant of the other, each condemning the other as "unscriptural." But New Age does not even have common assumptions to share with its rivals. What it believes about Jesus, the Bible, and salvation is out-and-out heresy to the born-again Christians and the charismatics.

Is Linda unique in her ability to move from one mythic structure to the next? My experience tells me that she is not.

Messages from Above

Astral entities are no more reliable than most people! Remember, the fact that astral beings can do things most of us cannot, like read minds, doesn't make them necessarily wise. . . .

Don't be misled into thinking that anyone who closes his eyes and begins speaking convoluted English is necessarily in touch with some wise being.

—J. Donald Walters, *How to Channel*

Glendower: I can call spirits from the vasty deep.
Hotspur: Why, so can I, or so can any man; But will they come when you call for them?

—William Shakespeare, *First Part of King Henry IV*, Act III, Scene I.

Psychic Counselors at the Faire

Much of New Age serves as alternative forms of counseling. The problems brought to channelers, psychics, and tarot card readers are not very different from those posed by the clients of psychiatrists, psychologists, and social workers. The major problems articulated are loneliness, depression, fear of the future, how to find a spouse, how to enhance a relationship, and how to get along with the boss.

The nitty-gritty "how to" questions are more commonly asked by the clients of psychics than by the patients of therapists, but the expectations that money can be exchanged for helpful advice are about the same.

About once a month, I attend the "Psychic Faires" regularly held at motels, shopping malls, gem shops, or other public places in various parts of northern California. As common as Tupperware parties in my area, such gatherings offer a smorgasbord of New Age practitioners. A typical "faire" is set up by an entrepreneur, who advertises, sets up the tables or booths, collects the entrance fees, and sells strips of tickets, each of which is valid for a mini-session with one of the participating practitioners. At the end of the weekend, the sponsor splits the proceeds with the "artists."

It is my wont to wander about, eavesdropping on the various consultations and engaging the participants in conversation. Faires consist of a dozen to twenty "psychics." (In the next few pages, I shall use the term *psychic*, as the faire promoters do, to refer indiscriminately to all the practitioners regardless of their idiosyncratic talents). Larger regional meetings, such as the Whole Life Expo, attract tens of thousands of the curious to the booths of numerous service providers/merchants and to the lectures of more than a hundred New Age celebrities.

The booths and tables of the local faires are the domain of lesser known practitioners, each of whom is eager to build up a local clientele. Many of these psychics are unimpressive amateurs, attempting to make the transition from hobbyist to professional.

As I meander among the booths, I discover a concern among the full-time psychics for credentials and certification as a way of separating themselves from the teeming bumblers. Since there are hundreds of institutions in California alone that offer degrees and certificates in Aquarian arts and sciences, ranging from acupuncture to whole-brain learning, it is not difficult to obtain some sort of credential. In the spring issue of *Common Ground,* a New Age directory for the San Francisco area, ninety-six programs advertise under the heading of "certification & degrees." The most common certification is in hypnosis, and is earned by attending a fifty-five-hour course. Also in evidence at about half the booths are certificates of ordination from mail order mills, such as the Universal Life Church.

The channelers, psychic readers, tarot card experts, and other advice givers are quite defensive about the issue of certification. Although I have never raised it as an issue in any of my impromptu interviews at the faires, I am often shown diplomas and other official-looking documents. I fully expect to meet the Scarecrow, displaying a sheepskin and reciting the Pythagorean Theorem.

When I engage them in conversation, another form of certification immediately arises: experience. The average psychic, who is a woman in her forties, has always known she was a psychic. She is the product of a long line of psychics or healers. Her mother was a pious churchgoer. When the psychic-to-be was about six or ten, she started having strange experiences. She could predict the future, find lost objects, and levitate her dolls. While her parents and her playmates' parents may have been negative, her other female relatives, particularly a grandmother or an aunt, were interested and supportive. Perhaps this relative had similar experiences or had a mother who was famous for her psychic abilities. At puberty, the psychic's gift seemed to abate.

After she was married and had a few children, the typical psychic's consciousness became deluged with those almost forgotten states from her youth. Her friends began coming to her for advice. In response, she issued dire warnings and hopeful forecasts. Her predictions proved accurate, and her reputation grew, but her husband became emotionally remote or abusive. Soon her first marriage ended. Scant months later, she married again. Her second husband was as practical and businesslike as she was ethereal. The second marriage lasted only a few years. She should have known better than to have married a Capricorn, she laments.

The other area of sensitivity has to do with the psychics' fear of traditional religion. They assume that all Christians are fundamentalists and that all fundamentalists are witch-baiters. Several psychics report that they have been picketed, insulted, assaulted, and otherwise intimidated by "Christians." Some of them have told me that they have unlisted phone numbers, accept new clients only by referral from their friends, and keep relatively low profiles in their home communities because of the New Age bashers.

At the last four faires I attended, 75 to 90 percent of the psychics were women, which corresponds almost exactly with the composition of the faire attendees. The run-of-the-mill practitioners are rather unimpressive. Their educational attainments are low, their dress and general appearance rather run-down. Most of the women wear too much makeup and weigh themselves down with gaudy costume jewelry. Their conversation is hackneyed, cliché ridden, and ungrammatical—whether they are talking about metaphysics or making small talk. When I hear them interact with their paying customers, I find their advice shallow, unspecific, inappropriate, and unimpressive. While some of them are excellent intuitive counselors, the majority lack the most rudimentary skills. The fundamental weakness of psychics as counselors is that they never listen. They already know. So they talk, talk, talk. . . .

About 10 percent of the psychics are sophisticated, engaging, and impressive individuals. They understand themselves and their motivations. They are talented in being supportive listeners and advisers—whatever their particular tools may be. Their background seems to be in organized groups, such as Spiritualism, Theosophy, Anthroposophy, or Unity School of Christianity.

I have met only one happily married psychic. It is a standing joke among New Age practitioners that they are able to solve their clients' problems and help others to become rich and happy, but that their personal lives are disasters. It would be interesting to do statistical comparisons of the marital histories of psychics and ministers or of psychics and mental health professionals.

Looking for a Competent Psychic

Established, successful psychics are never seen at the local faires. They do not need the exposure and do not associate themselves with the up-and-coming. Wanting to interview a competent psychic, I went to my favorite occult bookstore for a recommendation. There I spied a folder of business cards of various healers, channelers, body workers, crystal healers, and other New Age practitioners. With no formal plan for using them, I took one of each. When I examined them a week later, one card seemed to stand out. Perhaps it was the attractiveness of the design or the vibrancy of the purple ink. After some prompting from my wife, I phoned Sande Sharlat, whose card described her as both a rebirther and a channel.

Without the usual "who are you and what terrible things are you going to say about us?" defensiveness, Sande said that an interview "sounds like fun" and agreed to meet my wife and me at a local coffee house. As per her description, Sande is about five feet tall and slim. Her lustrous curly brown hair frames a thin, oval face. Her complexion is clear and smooth; her eyes are dark brown and never seem to blink. Like many of the followers of the New Age I have met in university towns (but unlike most of the professional psychics I have met), Sande is well educated. Her upper middle class, suburban family sent her to the finest colleges, and she has a degree in music.

Her major occupation is as a rebirther, or "Vivation professional." As Sande explained it, rebirthing combines deep breathing exercises with a determined focusing on "subtle body talking." A rebirther guides the client to concentrate on the physical feeling that accompanies each emotional state, to "be with the sensation here and now," and "to make a place for the feeling in one's life."

Sande charges her clients seventy-five dollars for an initial session, which lasts two and one-half hours. She suggests that they follow up with nine additional sessions at intervals of not more than two weeks. After these sessions, Sande recommends that the client repeat the process with a male rebirther.

To become a rebirther, one must complete ten sessions with both a male and a female rebirther, practice the daily "affirmations" suggested by the rebirthers, and attend trainings offered by such "official" rebirthing associations as the International Vivation Community (headed by rebirthing founders Jim and Anne Leonard) or Loving Relationship Training (directed by Sondra Ray). A year prior to our meeting, Sande and more than five hundred rebirthers had attended an international training in Hawaii.

She told me that she teaches her clients "to learn to welcome all the weird feelings, to notice what they feel like in the body. As a rebirther, I have to be able to read energy."

I asked her what the outcome of the session usually was. She said: "The end is peace and bliss. But people get real irritable if they don't finish"—that is, if a particular session ends without a sense of resolution. She added: "Rebirthing works a lot faster than just counseling. The process is more a letting go of what you're not than an adding of new things."

She expressed her philosophy: "Every day is a new day to live—not a day closer to death. Rebirthing teaches a physical immortality. You have to beware of empowering your death urge; learn to empower your life urge."

As we sipped a second round of soft drinks, she went on: "Forgiveness is essential. Unconditional love is blocked inside of you. It hurts you, and it hurts the person you are not loving. You have to open up the channel of love. Forgiveness is acceptance or integration. It's coming to peace with what is there—not with what you wish you were."

She explained her process: "I use affirmations and visualizations. The point is: No one ever hurts you—they teach you things."

Without the slightest change in her facial expression or tone of voice, Sande suddenly shifted gears. "I'm going to step into the channeling stuff," she said. "I deal with it gently—in layers." Once the rebirthing process has located the pains and blockages, Sande lets her channeled personality give direction to the client. She later told me that she usually does either rebirthing or channeling sessions with a given client.

Suddenly the topic doubled back to rebirthing and forgiveness. "As a rebirther, I don't need to add any intensity to my clients' feelings of anger or resentment. I need to guide them to the gentlest, safest place, to let them know that if you create your reality, then no one can hurt you, that whatever happens, happens for you. Eventually they will see it and not blame themselves."

I asked her what specific techniques she used to enable her clients to let go of hatred and resentment. She replied: "I use the 'forgiveness diet,' which I learned from Sondra Ray. It's a written affirmation process, based on the teaching of Jesus about how many times one should forgive [one's] brother. Seventy times a day for seventy days, I have the client write: 'I forgive (name of person) completely. I divide the page into two columns. Thirty-five times a day for seven days, I have the client write 'I forgive (name of person) completely' in the first column and the first thing that comes to mind in the second column."

"But," I wondered aloud, "what happens when your clients resist you, when they refuse to do what you prescribe?"

Her response: "When I'm in resistance, my clients are in resistance. And besides, I have regular weekly support groups for my clients. I see all of my clients as parts of myself.

The more I own up to that, the better I am professionally. And if I can know who I am, I can know God."

Not wanting Sande's earlier reference to channeling to get lost, I asked her to tell me about it. Channeling, she feels, is the development of an intuitive power that was always there. She stated: "I've been writing music all my life—playing piano since age three. I always knew that the music was coming through me. I was always incredibly intuitive. My father started doing Transcendental Meditation when I was seventeen. He encouraged my sisters and me to join him. When I started doing TM, I was getting psychic."

At age twenty-six, Sande started pursuing *The Course in Miracles* while also engaged in rebirthing. While reading one day, the words, "Just listen," seemed to leap out at her. When she did listen, she heard a voice—"some very loving message."

"What did you do then?" I asked.

"I devised a method," she declared, "whereby I could get past the everyday noise—the chatter in my mind. The voice sounds like thinking. But it felt different. It would fill me up with love, and I would start shaking with energy and terror." She related that she would channel under the covers at night.

Her boyfriend, Tom, had read widely about channeling. "If he reads something, I'll dream it," she noted. At first, Sande felt quite a bit of resistance to the voice, but Tom reassured and encouraged her. Her entity has a name, "Hera," but Sande is not sure that the name really fits. Sometimes, she explained, she thinks of Hera as more of a committee than a single personality. Sande started doing channeling sessions for Tom and gradually introduced channeling into her lecturing and rebirthing sessions. She stated that she is a conscious channel, that she does not go into a trance or an altered state of consciousness, that sometimes the messages are spoken and sometimes written.

Impulsively, I thrust my legal pad and pen across the table to her. "Here," I said. "Show me."

After a moment's hesitation, she took up the pen and began to write. From time to time, I could see the words forming in her lips and jaw muscles. She wrote rapidly, looking up to comment from time to time. For instance, when she misspelled my name as "Lovell," she asserted, "This is deliberate. It means "one who is loved." The entire text of her written message to me is as follows:

> Good day, Lovell. Know that you are loved! You would like to distance yourself from this information you are gathering in an attempt to be safe. Being "different" has served you in the past by putting distance between you and other people. You actually would rather be different than loved. Is there anyone who really knows who you are? Your fear keeps yourself imprisoned inside the self. Ask your wife "Do you know me?" And in truth, she would only answer—"No! Not fully!"

It had taken Sande about a minute to write this. She informed us that sessions in which she channels usually last an hour or two. Her entity, Hera, she maintains, "has been a person, who is not now. Hera is my interpreter. I get the sense of a group of 'not people'—information. Hera is a teacher." She believes that through her Hera is writing "a user's manual for the human being." She described a weekly class led by Hera: "The topics come spontaneously. I just sit on the side and watch."

Sande started to tell me that "relationships are mirrors. Connie is you." She seemed antsy and uncomfortable, and explained that the channeling had left her "energized," that it was hard for her to stop.

So I suggested that we continue, and that she allow her spirit guide to speak to us. In a few minutes, we found an empty reading room at a nearby school and prepared to hear what Hera had to say.

In her Hera persona, the somewhat shy, self-conscious, and apologetic Sande becomes a powerful, centered, and prodigious presence with just the hint of an Indian accent. Sande is polite and tentative. Hera is smug and direct. The principal ground rule for dialogue with Hera is that neither party need worry about the feelings of the other. Since it is Hera and not Sande who is speaking, there is no reason for Sande to censor anything that she says or attempt to be tactful. Conversely, since it is a disembodied essence rather than a person that the subject is conversing with, the subject need not worry about Sande's tender sensibilities.

Depending on one's point of view, it may be said that a great deal of freedom arises from the ground rules or that there is incredible room for self-deception, manipulation, and inappropriate advice. Something in me resists the notion that I am another person's mirror or that a total stranger knows enough about me to give me advice. And that feeling was not dispelled by what Hera had to say.

Hera told me that I needed to realize that "I am enough." She asked me to ask myself "What are the ways I have overcompensated or proved I am not enough?" She recommended a visualization for my daily use: "Tell yourself to imagine for thirty seconds or a minute what I would be like if I were enough." And she urged me to "affirm daily: 'I am enough.' Write down all your negative thoughts in order to integrate them." Her final advice: "Just know that you are loved. It is okay to laugh now and then. Create with lightness and laughter. Remember that struggle is your choice and not a necessity."

Hera also had advice for my wife. She told Connie that she was refusing to acknowledge just how beautiful and powerful she really is. She recommended that Connie take a mirror and look at one of her features, such as her eyes, and repeat "I am beautiful" to herself.

When the Hera persona was dismissed, Sande asserted, "I am sad." I wanted to ask why, but knew that there would be no answer. What is is. It happens. That is all that it means. (I was learning!)

Did I feel that I had gained any great insight or new awareness as the result of my written and oral communications from Hera? My sense was that Sande is a very introspective and sensitive person and that because she knows her own inner processes and mind games so well, she is able to project them on others whose experience is similar. I think that much of her written message came out of her own anxiety about this stranger who was writing about her and who might not have entirely positive things to say. Nevertheless, I thought about what she had to say for days. I was bothered by the notion that I have made myself different in order to protect myself from being known and loved. A few days later, I told a group of ministers, who are my friends, about Hera and showed them the message. What I said to them is what I still believe: "I am different. I have always known that. Sometimes that's good, and sometimes it isn't. As a convert to Christianity, I am different from what I would have been if I had not converted. As a questing spiritual human being, I am different from religious persons who already have all the answers. As a blend of (a) practical, get-the-job-done pragmatist, (b) scholarly, I'd-like-to-think-about-it-for-a-while thinker, and (c) believer/seeker/worshiper/mystic, like Popeye 'I yam what I yam, and that's what I yam.'"

If I am different, my sense is that it is because I am different, not that I want to be different, seek to be different, or am different for any specific purpose. A psychic who teaches people to respect what is rather than mope about what ought to be or what could have been should have known that!

I guess I am doing exactly what Hera/Sande would want me to do. I am getting acquainted with myself, loving myself, and refusing to allow anyone else to dictate my reality. And that feels great!

CHAPTER SEVEN

The Witches of Salem

There is a way of life that is as old as humankind; yet, it began only yesterday. There is a religion that is as New Age as any Aquarian manifestation, but it will never admit it. The name of this path is *Wicca*. Its more familiar designation is Witchcraft.[1] I find Wicca to be the most typical of all of New Age's disorganized organizations. Ideologically and practically, Witchcraft is panentheistic, ecological, transformative, ecstatic, and tolerant. In addition, it is devoted to balancing masculine and feminine aspects of reality, honoring the arcane wisdom of other times and places, and affirming life. More than any other New Age phenomenon, it labors to overcome a horrific reputation. Despite its fluidity and inner tensions, the Crafte is a wonderful illustration of just how New Age works at the local level as well as the manner in which disparate local manifestations weave themselves together into a community of mutual concerns.

To use the word *Witch* is to summon up all manner of images derived from Halloweens past, fairy tales, TV sitcoms (above all "Bewitched"), and motion pictures, ranging from *The Wizard of Oz* and *I Married a Witch* to *Burn, Witch, Burn* and *The Witches of Eastwick*. Some Witches from our popular fantasies have green skin, warts, fly on broomsticks, and snack on little children. Others capriciously twitch their noses or wave their wands to assist, perplex, and entertain mere mortals. Some put their hexes on whomever displeases them. Others use their arts to heal sick bodies and broken hearts, to discern the future, and to repel the works of evil.

Which Way to the Witch Store?

Even before I had read my first book on Witchcraft or had conducted my first interview with a follower of Wicca, I had convinced myself that if I wanted to know something other than such fantasies, I must go to Salem, Massachusetts, where Witches had once, in the minds of the populace, been more than colorful tales. On a partly sunny Sunday, during a much appreciated, but all too temporary break in the summer heat, my wife and I drove to Salem, the infamous city of the 1692 Witch trials. We headed for the Witch Museum, where we witnessed a half-hour, larger-than-life diorama show. It was well produced and, for the most part, historically accurate. But we were disappointed that the presentation deliberately confused Witchcraft and Satanism (the same confusion that had gotten twenty people killed in the Massachusetts Bay Colony).

Wanting to tell someone about the errors perpetuated by the show, I struck up a conversation with a guide at the museum. Learning of my interest, she recommended that I attend a meeting of the local Spiritualist church. She explained that the minister calls on individuals at random from the audience and offers them communications from loved ones "on the other side." A few years ago, the guide reported, the minister told her that someone with "scratched knees and elbows" had a message for her. She knew that this was a reference to her daughter, who had died before her third birthday. She was not impressed by this trivial bit of information and refused to participate further. On another visit to the church, she was accompanied by her younger daughter. The minister told the daughter that someone wanted to speak to her and that this someone had in the past teased her by scratching her neck. The daughter was sure that this must be her father, who had died when she was nineteen. Having come to Salem not to commune with my own departed loved ones but to learn of earlier times, I asked for directions to the Peabody Museum and departed.

As my wife and I wandered down a narrow street on the way to the Peabody Museum (a collection of everything imaginable that the sea captains of Salem had brought back from the Far East in the eighteenth and nineteenth centuries), we happened to notice a tiny "Witch shop." We had accidentally stumbled on Crow Haven Corner, headquarters for Laurie Cabot, Salem's official Witch. Here was a door I could not but enter, and, there, in a minute, was the black clad Witch herself, her large eyes heavily accentuated with makeup, her wispy black hair seeming to reach out in all directions. I introduced myself, parried some suspicious questions, and made arrangements to talk to her the next day.

Laurie, whom I had seen in recent years on TV shows and in magazines, is chairperson of the Witches' League for Public Awareness, which she describes as "the Witches' anti-defamation league." She refers to her own path as "Witchcraft as a science." It is, she asserts, "compatible with all religious beliefs." She maintains:

> One can be a Witch and be a Christian—a Methodist—a Catholic—even a bishop! Witchcraft as a science underlies all religious beliefs, all psychic phenomena, and prayer. It is spell projection. Humans are responsible for themselves and for all living things. The Law of Witchcraft as a science is "Do what thou wilt and harm no living thing." We believe that the God or the Goddess lives within all things. Because we believe this, Witches are responsible for every thought and action.

She denied that they would ever slaughter goats or "do any of those things of which we have been accused." Laurie adamantly insisted that no version of Witchcraft ever had anything to do with Satan or evil spells. She and the more than twenty Witches with whom I spoke and/or corresponded during the summer of 1988 were in total agreement on this point. As she maintains: "Satan and evil belong to Christianity. They are the church's problem—not ours. Witchcraft is thousands of years older than Christianity."

She is greatly concerned about the stereotyped depictions

of Witches and Witchcraft in the media and in the arts. "Jim Henson [of the Muppets] is making a movie based on Roald Dahl's book *Witches*, which will set us back four hundred years." She recounted ugly encounters with fundamentalist Christians, who over the years discriminated against her. She elucidates: "They handed out all sorts of ugly literature, full of Bible quotes like 'Thou shalt not suffer a Witch to live in the land'—that sort of thing." Just a few days before my visit, she told me, a group of fundamentalist Christians from a neighboring town had announced that they were going to drive out the Witches' spirits through their superior spiritual powers. The boast of the fundamentalists and the reply of the Witches had been reported in the *Salem Evening News.*

Laurie is also distressed by the propaganda war being waged against "the old religion" by fundamentalist police officers. She spoke of a man who distributes a collection of anti-Witch materials known as "File 18." The (are we allowed to say?) specter of law enforcement officers with guns attempting to ferret out Witches is deeply unsettling to the Witches' League, Laurie reported. "Fortunately," she declared, "we have Witches who are police officers all over the country. Under the tradition of Witchcraft as a science, which I founded, there are Christian covens."

Other Wiccan Voices

Through Laurie and the Witches' League, I was able to make contact with many practitioners of "the Crafte" from coast to coast. I soon learned that Witchcraft is as divided as Christendom. A few basic convictions and attitudes bind Witches together in an extremely nondogmatic and loosely structured movement, which contains many distinct schools or traditions. None of the Witches was totally in accord with Laurie. Most took exception to what she had told me. For example, Judy Harrow wrote:

As I understand it, Laurie's "Witchcraft as a Science" concept refers to psychic development. While that may be compatible with any other religion, Witchcraft as a religion is polytheistic—and so is not compatible with monotheistic belief systems. Some Witches do honor Jesus or Mary along with other deities, but I doubt this would be acceptable to any Church.

Puck, a male Witch from metropolitan New York, adds:

I do not think Witchcraft is compatible with all religious beliefs. It is true that Wicca is not an exclusivistic religion, but it does have a set of beliefs—beliefs which I personally feel are incompatible with monotheism in any form.

There are people who worship Jesus as one among the gods, but no more so than Osiris or Lugh. . . . I personally would never invoke Jesus Christ in a ritual, but I would not stigmatize someone who would. In this sense only, Christianity is compatible with Wicca.

Jehana Silverwing of Connecticut states: "While I am in agreement with Laurie Cabot's statement that Witchcraft has nothing to do with Satan or evil spirits, Witchcraft to me is more than a science—it is, indeed, for me, in itself a religion and a philosophy of life which draws upon the intuitive and sacred as much as it does upon the logical, scientific side of existence."

Some Wiccans were eager to disown Laurie completely, declaring her an ersatz Witch and more of a media creation than a genuine practitioner of any of the Crafte's traditions. Few of them took the Jim Henson threat seriously, trusting his representations that Witches would not be defamed in his film. As Puck observes: "Nothing has the power to set us back four hundred years!"

A Look at Wicca

As I learned from dozens of conversations with Witches, from letters and information packets sent to me from various covens and Witch-awareness organizations, and from my electronic travels between far-flung computer bulletin board systems (BBSs), Wicca (the name preferred by most Witches for their religion) and related Nature or Goddess worship are endemic. While Witches are comfortable being classified as "neo-pagan," they object to the designation "New Age." Justificus asserts: "With all due respect to the term *New Age*, the Crafte is not so new. It has been estimated from cave drawings, old manuscripts, and other sources to be at least twenty thousand years old." Some Witches agree with him; others do not. The "Crafte" may indeed be ancient, but few living Witches can trace the lineage of the schools to which they belong more than a few decades. Contemporary Wicca was, according to the varying judgments of Wiccans themselves, rediscovered or reinvented by scholar-zealots in fairly recent times. Typical of many of the letters I received on the issue of the alleged ancient lineage of contemporary Witchcraft was one from Beth A. Pollen of Connecticut, who maintains:

> Some groups, Covens if you will, can trace their tradition back to before the burning times. Some of these groups chose to remain secretive because of tradition and/or fear of societal retribution. I cannot show you incontrovertible proof that traditional Covens with pre-burning times lineage exist, but neither can it be proven beyond a shadow of a doubt that they do not. It doesn't make sense to me that a new religious tradition like Christianity could survive its first few centuries of massive persecution and the well established religion of Witchcraft should be totally wiped out by a couple of centuries of persecution.

But does not Beth's appeal to "the well established religion of Witchcraft" beg the issue? Writing in the *Encyclopaedia Britannica*, M. G. Marwick rejects the basis of Beth's argument. Contemporary Witches, he contends, are not entitled to use the designation Witchcraft. He explains:

> The incorrect use of the term refers to persons claiming to be witches who are reported to belong to covens, to assemble

on appropriate calendrical occasions for sabbats at which the
coven leaders claim descent from earlier witches. This kind of
"witchcraft" . . . seems   highly   respectable. . . . These   so-
called witches claim to be adherents of an ancient religion, the
one to which Christianity is regarded as a counterreligion, and
in this way they seek to secure public recognition of their
eccentric activities by appealing to the cherished modern
value of religious toleration.

These practitioners usually turn out to be entirely sincere
but misguided.[2]

Witchcraft's elder statesperson, Doreen Valiente, asserts: "I
think our present-day rituals bear the same sort of relationship to
the ancient days that, for instance, the Sacrifice of the Mass in a
present-day cathedral bears to the little ritual meal that took place
under dramatic circumstances in the upper room of a tavern in
Palestine somewhere about 33 A.D."[3] Seventy percent of the
Witches I encountered are first-generation Wiccans; thirty
percent are the children of Witches. As Puck explains, Wicca is
"the modern reconstruction of the religions of tribal Europe,
stamped out so effectively in the Burning Times that no tradition
of the modern Crafte can legitimately claim to trace lineage
directly back to pre-Burning Times religion." To quote Valiente
again:

Well, to paraphrase Gertrude Stein, "a witch is a witch is a
witch is a witch." If someone is genuinely devoted to the ways
of the Old Gods and the magic of nature, in my eyes they're
valid, especially if they can use the witch powers. In other
words, it isn't what people know, it's what they are.[4]

Of the dozens of contacts I made via the "New Age" BBSs,
virtually all were with neo-pagans or followers of Wicca. In
simplest terms, the Witch faction dominates the electronic
New Age network. On one BBS, I found a brief Wiccan
creed:

BELIEFS AND CUSTOMS OF WICCA

Not every Wiccan will subscribe to all of these points, but generally they are representative.

1. The divine Spirit is present in all creatures and things: people, animals, plants, stones. . . .

2. The ultimate creative force manifests in both feminine and masculine modes; therefore it is often symbolized as The Goddess and The God.

3. In some covens, both are celebrated equally. In others, The Goddess is given precedence or even celebrated without reference to the God.

4. All Goddesses and Gods are aspects of The Goddess and The God. The aspects most popular in Wicca are the Triple Goddess of the Moon (Maiden, Mother, and Crone) and the Horned God of death and rebirth.[5]

5. Reincarnation and karma are valid concepts. Upon death one goes to a state of rest and reflection, and eventually chooses where and when s/he will be reborn.

6. Magick is practiced for positive (helping) purposes: spiritual development, healing, guidance, safety, etc.

7. Rituals are generally performed outdoors when possible, at the New and Full Moons, and at eight Sabbat festivals which mark the progression of the seasons.

8. Magick and celebration are performed in small groups, usually 3 to 13, called covens. These are basically autonomous—there is no central church authority or hierarchy.

9. There is no holy book, or prophet, no equivalent of the Bible or Jesus or Mohammed. Individuals have access to the divine and do not require an intermediary. Every initiate is regarded as a priest/ess.

10. The central ethic is "And ye harm none, do as ye will." Whatever energy you send out returns threefold, so it is wise to be kind to others. [Judy Harrow relates: "The Wiccan Rede is actually: 'An it harm none, do as ye will.' *Rede* is archaic for 'advice.' *An* is archaic for 'if.' So, in modern English: 'If it harms none, do as you will.' "]

11. We should live in harmony with the Earth and Nature, and not exploit them.
12. Though Wicca is a valid spiritual path, it is not the only one. There is no recruiting, and people should be free to choose the path that best fits their needs.
13. The concepts of original sin, sacrifice, redemption, confession, the divinity of Jesus, sinfulness of sex, Judgment, Heaven and Hell, denigration of women, bodily resurrection, and the Bible as divine revelation are not part of Wicca. Neither are Satanism, the Black Mass, desecration of cemeteries, the sacrifice of animals, etc.[6]

Judy Harrow adds her definition of Witchcraft:

Witches are priestesses and priests, people who have made the loving reconstruction of the Shamanic religion of tribal Europe one of the main focuses of our lives and our creative energies. For us, there are three main theological points:

1. Polytheism—validates the goodness of diversity. In a time when people of many cultures live and work together and when each individual must play many roles, polytheism can be a path of inner and outer peace.
2. Immanence—the belief that the Sacred is to be found within this life on this Earth, here and now. This teaches us to live and protect Nature and to create a situational ethic, based on human needs rather than authoritarian abstractions.
3. God/dess worship—an aspect of polytheism that specifically validates the sacredness of both genders.

Puck adds that "Wicca is basically a religion of nature worship, whose central deity is the Earth Herself. Gaia (as she is called) is the only deity whose existence has been verified by modern science—although, of course, her divinity is still a matter of disagreement."

Women's Separatists Within the Crafte

From various parts of the country, I have reports of
Christians, particularly women, who have left traditional
churches and joined semi-organized neo-pagan or Wiccan
groups. Their groups are usually for women only and are
viewed by many Witches as "the women's separatist community within the Crafte." As Judy Harrow argues: "Men are
very much a part of mainstream Wicca. My own tradition or
denomination, Gardnerian, requires a High Priestess and a
High Priest to lead a coven. Our emphasis is on balance and
equality." My conversations and correspondence with male
Witches throughout North America confirm Judy's opinion.[7]

Typical of the separatists is Maya, a bright and witty
seminarian in New England. Shortly after we met, Maya told me:
"I'd rather carry a rock in my pocket to remind me of Mother
Earth than wear a cross around my neck as a symbol of violence."
The young woman is a lesbian from a fundamentalist home. For
her, the Wiccan community was a place of refuge and
affirmation. In Wiccan rituals, she finds validation "as a woman
and as a full, nonmarginalized member of humanity." It is not
merely that the Wiccan community is accepting of her, but that
through its rituals she feels attuned to her own body and to the
earth from which she has sprung and in which she remains
rooted. Also, as her remark suggests, Wicca's recognition that the
female is as essential as the male provides a basis for her protest
against male dominance and exploitation of women and all the
havoc that patriarchy has wrought when writ large upon human
relationships, whether they are societal, economic, or geopoliti-
cal.

For thousands of women, Wicca represents ritual and
ideology to counterbalance what they perceive to be the
sexism of Judeo-Christian religions. "The bias against
women is so deep and pervasive," one observer told me, "that
no tokenism—not the adoption of inclusive rather than
masculine language in the liturgy and the hymnal or the

religious defamation. In addition, they are often held responsible by gossipy police and careless media sources for virtually every unsolved crime of a bizarre or heinous nature. Protesting the pressures that have forced the Crafte underground, Prairie Wind writes:

> I think it's time Witchcraft be accepted as a legitimate religion by the general public. I know of only one legal cemetery for Witches in this country. And I know of children who have to hide their religion. Witches marry, birth and bury in America. But for many of us our rites of passage must be done in secret. . . . And I can't help but wonder how many people are out there—young and old—who were born Witches but because of the fear instilled by hate propaganda or isolation will never have a "homecoming." That's very, very sad.

2. The refusal of neo-paganism to recognize or respect any dualism between body and soul is upsetting to the ascetic types in traditional religions. The worship of the neo-pagan celebrates the body and the senses; the ascetic represses them as distractions to the spiritual life.

3. The tendency of neo-paganism to view nature as sacred rather than as inferior to humans and something to be conquered by humans undermines the masculine/patriarchal perspective of Western theism. Our competitive, frenzied, industrialized way of life seems to be challenged by the neo-pagan quest for "at-one-ment" with nature.

4. The neo-pagan celebration of the individual will and the lack of a sense of guilt as a motivating factor in human behavior undermine traditional Christian ethics. In addition, neo-paganism relies on rituals, spells, and other psychic means in order to achieve the ends of the individual will. Judy Harrow states: "Actually, our rituals are a powerful psychological technology for focusing and directing the deep mind. One common definition: 'Magic is the art of changing consciousness in accordance with will' [Dion Fortune]."

For traditionalists, such means are but superstition and

ordination of women or even the retranslation of the Bible to remove its anti-feminine bias—can undo centuries of refusal to regard women as human beings fully made in the image of God. The answer is that women should worship the divine Mother as well as the Heavenly Father, that they should adopt or develop rituals suited to themselves as Nature's co-creators and protectors." As Maya states:

> It's not that we necessarily want to worship God as Mother. It's that those who worship God as Father perpetuate violence against women. And for such people to say that I'm made in God's image means that we must perpetuate violence against women. And I don't want to be made in that image—I'm not that image. I'm not the reflection of God the Father, but rather God the Father is the creation of people who engage in war and violence. If I reflect God, then God is gentle—my God is just. My God is good and the concept of original sin or badness does not exist.

A somewhat different stance was taken by many Witches. For example, Judy Harrow insists:

> I personally think that there's a danger in relating to God or Goddess as parent, regardless of gender. This fosters dependency and "followership." I tend to relate to Goddess as sister and to God as lover.
>
> Further, not all Father God myths are warlike or violent. The Dagda (Irish) is a nurturing Father Provider.[8]

Comments Jehana Silverwing, "While those who deny that there are other ways of looking at deity than as 'God the Father' perpetuate violence against all, male or female, who at least wish to examine and explore other aspects of deity, worshiping God the Father does not in and of itself reflect war and violence and hatred of women."

Judy concludes, "Maya seems to be dangerously close to

substituting the 'patriarchy' with the 'matriarchy,' as if the 'matriarchy' can solve all ills."

For women who share Maya's pain and dislocatedness, the lure of the new paganism is powerful indeed. It is a way to recover the expressions of female power and female symbolism that have been all but extirpated in Western religion. As Carol P. Christ hypothesizes:

> Myths suppressed by the canonical traditions often contained powerful female symbolism; the texts or traditions transmitting this symbolism may often have had a special appeal for women because they offered greater opportunities for the expression of female power; and the persons persecuted by the canonical tradition may have been disproportionately female.[9]

In the traditions being developed by some of today's most conspicuous outsiders and heretics, the women in the women's spirituality movement and the feminist Witches, there is a resurgence of interest in female power and female symbolism.[10]   No doubt, the medieval Christian attack on Witches was an expression of male insecurity. Christianity had become a faith dominated by male priests. The presence in their respective parishes of powerful women was a threat to priestly authority. For centuries and centuries, Christianity had narrowed what was to be tolerated and permitted until it seemed to run like sand into the waist of an hourglass, there to be filtered through the village priest to whom the inheritors and practitioners of ancient folklore, most of them women, were a constant threat. According to the historians of Witchcraft, the priests had a difficult time dealing with powerful women for two reasons. First, the vitality of the women stirred the celibate priests to lust, feelings that they projected on the women. I think that explains why Witches were habitually accused of participating in sexual orgies and performing coitus with the devil. In addition, the presence of the folk practitioners at times of childbirth, illness, and death

made them a threat to the prestige of the priests. Pow women who saw the earth as the creation or co-creatior female deity, who rejected the dangerous male notior the supernatural is something apart from and abov natural, were more than the priests of Christendom bear. Such women were a threat to the very stabi! Christian civilization. As Joseph Campbell notes:

> Because [in Christianity] nature is thought of as corr every spontaneous act is sinful and must not be yielde You get a totally different civilization and a totally diffe way of living according to whether your myth presents n: as fallen or whether nature is in itself a manifestatic divinity, and the spirit is the revelation of the divinity t inherent in nature.[11]

A Religion Seeking Respect

As attractive as it may be for some, Witchcraft is the Dangerfield of contemporary religion. Its lament: "I do respect." Attempting to explain "why witches scare Naomi R. Goldenberg has presented several reasons in *Changing of the Gods: Feminism and the End of Traditional* Since I find Goldenberg's explanation useful, I have su it and added my comments as follows.

1. Female deities as an expression of divine r categorized by religionists and scholars of r: primitive, blasphemous, and evil. Inherent in sucl are value judgments arising from a masculine and ↿ point of view. But, it might be asked, why should th pre-industrial societies be called "primitive" when are as sophisticated as our own modern world ι why is it assumed that monotheism is ethically anc superior to polytheism?

Practitioners of Witchcraft report job discrimin isolation and shunning, violence to their p property, public ridicule, desecration of their h₍

degenerated magic. They are condemned not only as useless but also as evil, as expressions of the human will in rebellion against God, and as harmful.

5. Neo-paganism views time as circular and repetitive. Hence, it lacks the sense of crisis that is so important to traditionalists, for whom time is linear and never to be repeated. ("Only one life, 'twill soon be past. Only what's done for Christ will last.") Since many neo-pagans believe in reincarnation, they do not share the traditional Christians' sense of apocalyptic urgency. Nor do neo-pagans believe in heaven or hell. Rather they feel that there is an immediate justice, a karmic law, in the everyday world. In simplest terms, human beings reap what they sow—not in an afterlife, but here and now. As Jehana Silverwing explains:

> For some, karma is something which is worked out over several lifetimes. For others, reincarnation is not an important tenet of their religion—karmic "payback" or "debt" is valid within a lifetime. Karma is that which one brings upon herself by her actions. It does not go as far . . . as to blame victims—blame and guilt are aspects from culture at large in which we live that we seek to minimize . . . karma does involve recognizing your own responsibilities; living up to them; and being willing to accept/understand when your own violations of those responsibilities come back eventually to tap you on the head. Sometimes it [reality] taps hard.

6. Neo-paganism accepts the decay of the body as natural and inevitable. For traditionalists, it is depressing—the consequence of sin and the fall of humankind. Neo-paganism rejects the notion of original sin altogether. Like all natural phenomena, human beings are intrinsically neither good nor evil—what they are depends on what they do with the energies, talents, and abilities with which Nature has endowed them.

7. Neo-paganism sees no absolute gulf between good and evil. Any thing, event, or condition of human experience can

be used for good purposes, evil purposes, neutral purposes, or no purpose at all.

8. Neo-paganism reveres no text as sacred. It has no Bible. It is essentially pluralistic, revering a variety of traditions and disciplines. Hence, it has no written documents to study, which confounds both religion scholars and fundamentalist critics. It is amazing how often documents and scriptures are concocted just so the critics of neo-paganism will have something against which to direct their attacks. Commercializers of New Age phenomena have also contributed to the misrepresentation of neo-paganism by producing such texts as *The Satanic Bible*. Fundamentalist apologists have also contributed to the hatemongering directed against Witches by swallowing as factual the rantings of alleged high priests/esses who have become converts to evangelical Christianity.

9. Neo-paganism has no rigid law or discipline. It's live-and-let-live ethic seems to provide no basis for judging, condemning, punishing or ostracizing any within its community. Nor does it prescribe a particular path of spiritual devotion as binding on all members. However, since neo-paganism is a form of group behavior, the group influence may often actively prescribe or proscribe behavior through a process of consensus-building. In this way, each Wiccan coven becomes a society of mutual healing. Thus if I ask a Witch to define what a Witch is, he or she will usually reply, "I am a healer." As healers, Witches are likely to cut out the diseased and unhealthy. The credentials of Witches who exploit or harm fellow coven members can be revoked (and have been revoked) by other Priests or Priestesses within a given tradition.

10. Sexual behavior is not governed by elaborate restrictions. Neo-pagans contend that sex like most human activities has its own regulatory principles. Sex should not be governed by artificial restrictions. The basic law remains: do what you will as long as all parties are in agreement and you don't hurt anyone. Even though such general statements are often offered as a

one-sentence definition of Wiccan ethics, they are really too simple. Wicca says be responsible. Consider the consequences of your actions. Be aware of the power you have as a person in your relationships with other people and the power that other people have in their relationships with you. Mutuality—the ability to be who you are and to be connected with another for the benefit of both—is the key.

In our telephone conversations, Witches from several parts of the country spoke to me repeatedly of the "Threefold Law of Return": Whatever one does in this life, whether for good or for evil, will come back to that person threefold. So if one does good, one will receive good. If one does harm, one will be harmed.

For the most part, neo-paganism is accepting of gay and lesbian life-styles. In addition, it demands of its dominant heterosexual following that they not discriminate against gays and lesbians. Even though some Wiccans feel that homosexuality is a violation of the dictates of Nature, Wicca is generally a safe haven for gay spiritual seekers who have been spurned as misfits by traditional religious institutions.

11. Neo-pagan rituals are deeply serious, yet full of fun, spontaneity, play, and jokes. As Deborah Rozman, a longtime member of the northern California spiritual community, University of the Trees, exclaims: "Religion is heart connections and having fun. Sharing in the fun is the real holy communion."[13] Neo-pagan rituals celebrate life. The knowledge that they are invoking and connecting with fundamental power is the source of their seriousness. The fact that the ritual is for a particular group meeting at a particular time in a particular place (and not for all people everywhere) produces the gaiety and playfulness.[14] As Maya maintains, "The church celebrates a dead deity. Wicca celebrates birth, the living, people joining their lives together or unjoining themselves—the everyday stuff." How many traditional ritualists would permit such a combination of solemnity and sheer merriment?[15]

12. The separatistic tendencies of the so-called "Dianic," or

feminist, movement (which are highly controversial within Wicca) have attracted the scorn of even the Crafte's friendly critics within Christendom. A religion of women, by women, and for women, which neither excludes men nor gives them any special place, is quite consonant with the effort by women to reclaim their power in the contemporary world. However, as Presbyterian theologian Diane Tennis warns, womanspirit must be careful not to confuse the rebellion against male authority with the recovery of women's spirituality. Also exchanging a dependence on Father with a dependence on Mother may leave women as far removed from independence as ever.[16]

Is the divine Mother whom the religious feminists worship anything more than the traditional, male-revered and male-encouraged traits of nurturing and empowerment projected on the heavens? As Judy Harrow reminded me: "Yes, there is real danger that some of us may simply deify the old, stereotypical feminine gender role and box ourselves in even worse than before. This is one of my strongest reasons for steering clear of simple Mother-oriented monotheism. Some of us call that 'momotheism.' "

Moreover, Tennis is convinced that "any branch or brand of feminism that does not engage a larger community and does not move into political activity is an endangered species. Some womanspirit religions eschew the very kind of worldly power that could keep it alive."[17] That, I would add, would enable it to make a significant difference in the real world.

13. The fundamental problem faced by "the Crafte" is the bad press it has suffered for several centuries. The public confuses gentle practitioners of simple magic with creatures of popular mythology who reject God and orthodox doctrine, worship Satan and sign their souls over to him, sacrifice animals and infants, engage in orgies, and fly through the air on broomsticks. The failure to distinguish between (a) "the old religion," in which simple rituals are employed to assure good crops, healthy livestock, fertile

families, good health, prosperity, freedom from stress, and general well-being and (b) the almost entirely fictional entity portrayed as Witchcraft in the movies, theater, comic books, tabloids, and television is wrong and unjust, has been the source of incalculable human misery, and remains a continuing source of calamity.

Why a Witch Now?

Given the centuries of propaganda and the enduring prejudice against the Crafte, why should anyone in his or her right mind want to be known as a Witch at this time in history? This was the question I asked a number of Witches via correspondence, phone conversations, and computer bulletin boards. The Witches who spoke with me directly evidently could tell from my tone of voice that my question did not presuppose that Witches are not in their right minds. A few Witches who saw my question only in writing were offended and became highly defensive. The majority did not. A few of the replies I received are as follows:

> You have asked: "Why would anyone in his or her right mind want to be known as a Witch?"
> My reply: Well, if Witches are not really evil, then it's true that the problem may not be so much being a Witch as being known as a Witch. Maybe something is wrong when one cannot be known as a member of any nonviolent, genuine religion. Perhaps someone should do something about that!
> And, perhaps, aside from the strange folk, natural-born rebels, and those who seek out counter-culture lifestyles for the thrill—some rational people find that the risks of the Crafte are not out of proportion to the rewards. There was a time when the Wise Woman or Cunning Man—healer, sage, midwife, human almanac and practical psychologist—was needed and highly respected.
> —Justificus [a male Witch of the Alexandrian Tradition living in the Southwest], letter to the author, August 12, 1988.

Why would anyone call himself or herself a "Witch"?

There are two sayings that are practically clichés that answer your question.

1) Witches are born not made. I feel this applies to me and many of my friends. I attended Protestant churches on a regular basis, but it never "took." At an early age you realize you don't fit the norm. You have a different way of seeing things. Another thing is psychic experiences that you had as a child that the people around you don't understand. My parents bought a set of encyclopedias when I was in the 4th grade. In them I discovered the Greek & Roman pantheons. It was wonderful and it made sense to me! I read everything I could get my hands on. When I was 18 I got Doreen Valiente's book *An ABC of Witchcraft* from a book club. I was in shock. I finally realized I wasn't crazy—I was a "Witch"!!! . . . To discover that there were others out there who felt like me was beyond words.

Which brings us to cliché #2—I'd "come home." And that's exactly what it's like. You finally realize what you are and where you belong.

—Prairie Wind, woman member of a coven in the northern Great Plains area, letter to the author, August 2, 1988.

While I dabbled with Wicca for awhile, I was not convinced that I had found a home . . . until I attended Pan Pagan '80 in Indiana, a festival of at least 700 Witches and neopagans. I needed to be fully convinced that Wicca was indeed a "real" religion; that indeed it answered to real human needs while connecting to a real divinity. Convinced of its genuineness by way of that festival, I have been here ever since, growing and learning. The learning never ceases.

—Jehana Silverwing, Hearthstone Connections, Connecticut, letter to the author, August 30, 1988.

You pose the question: "Why would anyone in his or her right mind want to be known as a Witch?" If what the anti-Pagans have been saying about Witchcraft is true then no one in his or her right mind would. If what anti-Semitic groups have been saying about Jews were true then no one would want to be known as a Jew either. But what the Jews

have been accused of isn't true and they've fought long and hard for their rights. They're proud to be Jews. What we've been accused of isn't true either and I'm proud to be a Witch. As a police officer I've fought to preserve the freedoms which allow the anti-Pagans to freely and publicly express their fears about us. These same people want to deny *me* the same right. I won't be slandered. I want to reclaim the respect that the title Witch deserves.
—Constable Kerr Cuhulain, coordinator of the Wiccan Information Network, letter to the author, September 18, 1988. (Constable Cuhulain serves on the police liaison committee of the WITCH Society [Wiccans Invoking Tolerance, Compassion, and Harmony].)

Why would I want to be called a Witch?
First, because I have a strong sense of identification with the women and men who were killed in the Burning Times. . . .
In recent times I have begun to feel that the modern resurgence of Witchcraft may be due to the Goddess deciding that she needs us back, and timing the rebirths of people who died in the Burning Times to coincide with the time when she needs to be rescued from ecological murder.
I tried on the word Witch, and it fit. . . .
Saying "I am a Witch" makes me feel empowered, a feeling people contending with today's world desperately need.
—Puck, letter to the author, September 22, 1988.

The kind of Witchcraft that was persecuted by Catholic and Protestant authorities alike during and after the Reformation probably never existed except in the imaginations of the persecutors. The anti-Witch texts from the King James Version of the Old Testament, which were used to justify the hysteria of the seventeenth century and are still quoted today, are malicious distortions. The original Hebrew text contains terms whose meanings have been lost, which most certainly have nothing to do with the Nature religions of Europe or the neo-paganism of contemporary North America.
Once the purely fictitious version of Witchcraft had

become the object of rumormongering and speculation, no doubt a handful of rich, bored degenerates actually reenacted every despicable detail of the Witch hunters' fantasies just for the heck of it. On rare occasions, sociopaths and criminals in our own day play at being satanic Witches on their own. But to suggest, as some professional and amateur heresy hunters do, that such depredations are widespread is fallacious. The worst that one can say about today's Witches is that they are innocuous, that their spells and rituals are ineffectual. The best that one can say is that the Crafte is about healing, saving the planet, and celebrating holiness. Whatever contemporary pagans may be, they are harmless. The malice of the modern Witch hunters is not.

The Witches of Seminary X

Meeting the Witches of Salem and others at the seminary that Maya attends gave me a sense of just how much trouble the patriarchal God is in with feminists. For them, God the Father and God the Son belong to the repressive past. If such exclusivistic symbols for power are not dead, they ought to be. It is quite a shock to my system to learn that every time I utter the Lord's prayer ("Our Father"), I cast another stone at half the human race! Is there not some way of saving both sets of metaphors? Isn't it just as much a distortion of human nature to remove Father, Son, and Brother from our religious vocabulary as to overemphasize Father?

The Witches have uncovered a fundamental issue. Where there is a heavenly Father, there are likely to be dependence fantasies, authoritarianism, the insistence on conformity rather than independence, externally imposed ethical standards instead of the creation of one's own morality, and the demand for obedience rather than spontaneous service in love. How does one deal with this dilemma? Reject the whole theist system? Seek to transcend it as do the mystics and sages of many spiritual traditions? Or exchange Father for Mother as the exclusivistic Witches do?

Confusing to me are the attempts by some followers of Wicca to remain within the Christian church. For example, Maya is currently a seminary student. She hopes to be ordained to the ministry of her church. She wants to be accepted, even embraced, by the fellowship of Christians even though she cannot respect their irremediably patriarchal, anti-female symbolism. She knows that they cannot accept her reverence of the Great Mother. Yet, she pursues ordination, she explains, not only out of a sense of calling and mission, but as a way of being cleansed from the sense of pollution she carries with her as an incest victim. Somehow, she insists, if a bishop of her church embraces her despite her lesbianism, her feminism, and the sins inflicted on her in the past, she will be healed and transformed. Maya expects a great deal. Attempting to be both a Witch and a Christian, explains Judy Harrow, is for some people "a reflection of their own inner conflict and confusion." She adds: "For others, it is a thoughtful and loving attempt to build a new and more inclusive synthesis." And for still others, Judy maintains, because the church contains so many oppressed women, it is simply a good place to seek converts to feminism.

I am a bit more comfortable with Maya's friend and fellow Witch, Angie. I interviewed Angie in her office. She is working part-time as a research assistant while pursuing her second advanced degree in theology at a Protestant theological seminary. She also works part-time as a therapist. Angie grew up in the Roman Catholic Church. She related: "My father was a mystic. I was reared praying—communicating with God and feeling that he communicated with me."

In high school, she became involved in the charismatic movement. She studied theology in college and, she states, became obsessed with the question: "How does one live the gospel?" For six years, she was active in the Catholic Worker and the Catholic peace movements, participating in many acts of civil disobedience against nuclear weapons. At the time, she was "spiritually married" to a fellow worker. As a "political statement," they refused to undergo a conventional wedding ceremony.

The groups in which they did political work became divided, wrestling with the issue of feminism. "Reading Mary Daly's *Beyond God the Father* really turned me around," she recalls. In 1983 she went back to school, earning a degree in theology at a Midwestern seminary. During this time, she recounts, "I came out as a lesbian—reclaiming and recreating what it meant to be a woman." She felt a deep sense of "being guided by the Spirit and by the Goddess." She explained: "What the Goddess is all about is women experiencing liberation as women." She continued:

> I don't call myself a Christian anymore, even though my primary experience of Christianity is that it was liberating in many aspects of my life. I tell my friends, "Jesus was the door that led me right out of the sheepfold."

Yet, she continues to pursue her theology degree, finding the seminary one of few places in society where ultimate questions are still asked, and not wanting to throw away her background and experience.

> I don't experience liberation in the Christian community. Where I experience liberation is in gatherings of women. You cast a circle, and inside the circle you see what happens.

Angie feels that her life-style has made her a pariah within Christianity and within the dominant culture. She stated: "I have become spiritually and economically marginalized. I've never had a job making more than seven thousand dollars a year. What helps me to survive is that there is a lesbian community. Wherever I go, I can find housing—house-sharing with other women."

I changed the subject, asking her if her particular form of

Witchcraft had any absolute values. "Of course," she replied, "we *do* have absolutes. They are more political. The central question is always: How does this work for the liberation of women—and for the liberation of lesbian women? How does this work for the liberation of all people who are oppressed? Why do we use the word *Witch*?" she asked rhetorically. "Out of defiance. As a way of defying societal norms for women."

Angie clenched and unclenched her hand a few times as though she were grabbing her words from the air. She said:

> We use astrology, crystals, past lives because it's a way to talk to each other. It's whimsical. These are ideas to play with. They are alternate ways of talking. I've "prayed" for things, and they've happened. Likewise I've entered into relations with energies, with life. I put out something I might want. The more detached I am, the less worried and obsessed I am about something, the more likely it is to happen. I like this image: I send out my desire like an arrow. I need to send it out with whatever force I'm feeling, but also to let go of it.
>
> Worship is abandoning myself to reality, to the creator, life force, or the Goddess. Magic is that power that's used to make a change in the real world. I think of healing in that category. When I was a charismatic, I had a distinct sense of Jesus speaking to me, telling me to place my hand on my friend's head. It healed her.
>
> Power is frightening. How do we contain it? We can cast a circle, ritualize it. In fundamentalism, we turn it into dogma. What women can share is a particular mystery. What men can share is a particular mystery—but a different mystery. Our rites must be done in a women's-only group—to recover, rediscover that mystery. I want to be where God/Goddess is working, and that is among the marginalized. That's very exciting for me. I don't know if the world is getting worse or better, but I have hope.
>
> What's exciting is oppressed people striving to be free. Yet, things seem more and more oppressive. The big fight is not between the United States and Russia, but between the United States and Russia on the one hand and the Third World on the

other. I personally am not going to change the world. I have a little corner, and it feels important for me to be doing my work—being a therapist for lesbians and other marginalized women, pursuing the study of lesbian theology, being an "out" lesbian. I love the winter solstice, praying that the sun will come back. Somehow I know that my prayers do help the sun to come back. So does being a Lesbian, feminist, political activist.

I sympathize with Angie's sense of outrage. I have been marginalized at times in my own life as a Jew, a Jewish Christian, an ordained minister, a religion Ph.D., a liberal mystic, and even as an author. But I do not have a sense of being given permission to just be myself by Angie or Maya or any other of the lesbian Witches I have known. I am a man. They do not trust me. They must work out their own special magic as women without me. Perhaps in a century, when equality has been achieved, we will be able to talk to one another as equals; we will be able to stop accusing one another of not being able to understand; we will stop looking for things to be offended by; and we will get our minds off sexual rights issues and unite to save our planet. As a traditional Witch asserted in a recent conversation: "The liberation of Nature must come first. Sexual equality will not comfort us if we are choking in our poisons." Unfortunately, I do not have a hundred years—nor, I fear, does our world.

CHAPTER EIGHT

New Age Religious Experience

At the heart of New Age are ecstatic experiences, encounters with mystery, brooding intuitions, and strange imaginings. First come the powerful feeling states, penetrating one's soul like an unexpected, but impenetrable, fog. These states have no name and no content, but soon they attach themselves to symbol-pictures, images of the world as meaningfully related to the individual. Ultimately all religious rites, myths, statements, beliefs, and theologies arise from symbol-pictures. A person feels different, feels connected to something real or permanent. But such an awareness is vague, fluid, and tenuous. Somehow an image freezes the feeling in place and keeps it from evaporating.

Each of us exists in a time and place defined by family, society, economics, and history, from which we derive ideas, values, and attitudes—a virtual vocabulary and syntax of what can be experienced. The context in which we find ourselves conditions but does not predetermine what we shall feel, think, or do.

Religious or spiritual experiences can disrupt, confuse, and throw us off balance. Sometimes they just fade away; sometimes they attach themselves to symbol-pictures and shape our lives. As I reflect on the past, I am aware that from childhood my life has been dominated by three symbol-pictures: (1) the companionship of a friend who accepted me (evident in my experiences with Lars of Mars and in my fellowship with Jesus); (2) the presence of a monitor or judge, the ever-present, inner "Watchbird";[1] and (3) the comfort of resting on the bosom of the universe as part of the greater whole, an experience recaptured in nature, in dreams or daydreams, in the presence of comforting persons, such as my maternal grandmother.

Symbols are not arbitrary, but they are capricious. They are not consciously chosen. Rather, they emerge from and reflect an immediate awareness of the Real. Symbol-pictures cannot be refuted any more than the experiences from which they arise can be refuted. But once they have been translated into assertions, they are vulnerable to logical and historical criticism, and once they are translated into moral maxims they may turn out to be relevant or irrelevant to the convert's ongoing life.

Although symbol-pictures hide in our consciousness like half-forgotten dreams, they are more powerful and enduring than any doctrine or ethical maxims. Authoritarian religious personalities cannot deal with the ambiguity of symbol-pictures. So they translate them into rigid dogmas and rules. They fear imagination and openness to the real. They reduce the encounter with God to conformity. They set up fences to protect themselves and their followers from anything that cannot strictly be controlled. Their insecurity demands that their converts be exactly like them. Soon followers dress, talk, act, and think like their leaders. They share their leaders' prejudices, vices, and political leanings. Layer upon layer of custom, patterns of behavior, and misconception crush the original feeling states and obliterate the primal symbol-pictures.

Reducing the encounter with the Real to a handful of beliefs, social prejudices, and ethical norms takes only a few hours. Recapturing and interpreting a symbol-picture is a lifelong proposition, a vocation that is dangerous and unpredictable. Anything that fires the imagination—the arts, music, literature, or personal creativity—draws us close to the wellsprings of our encounter with the Real and the original symbol-pictures that there arose. Beliefs and norms nail down ephemeral experiences, guaranteeing that creativity will have results. But narrow creeds and strict rules are a poor substitute for the chaos of the life of the imagination.

In my studies of American religious experiences, I have found at least three major streams: natural, numinous, and mystical.

Natural Religious Experience

Organized manifestations of natural religious experience consist of identification with the processes, changes, and contingencies of nature. It expresses itself in rituals intended to restore the individual to the primal womb of Mother Earth, perhaps by sympathetic magic or by ecstatic states attained through drugs, dance, or chanting. Neo-paganism and Wicca strive after manifestations of this sense of undifferentiated unity with nature.

We may consider, for instance, the so-called primitive or pagan religions in which the line between subject and object, humanity and nature, creation and creator does not exist. The "primitive" consciousness experiences the cosmos as an organism from which the individual cannot be separated. Through the use of magic rites and rituals, primitive societies recreate the rhythms of the universe—rhythms in which they are continually involved. The primitive consciousness is concerned with cleaving to those patterns of individual and social behavior that express a unitary consciousness and in shunning those patterns that interfere with it.

Numinous Religious Experience

Numinous experience focuses on a transcendent being, who lures us to fellowship, yet pushes us away as unworthy. God reveals himself to us, fascinates us, and terrifies us. Numinous religion is preoccupied with taboo breaking and atonement, transgression and forgiveness. It tends to locate

God outside or above the world of nature and human affairs. It is typically patriarchal and authoritarian.

Mystical Religious Experience

Mystical religious experience differs from the numinous in several important respects. Subjectively, the mystical experience is characterized by a blissful intensity that surpasses and eludes description. The reality that produces these states is, as Evelyn Underhill (probably the best known student of mystical phenomena) notes, "still mediated . . . under symbols and forms." The variety of such symbols is enormous. The adoring gaze of the mystic, says Underhill, "now finds new life and significance in the appearances of nature, the creations of music and art, the imagery of religion and philosophy, and reality speaks to him through his own credal conceptions."[2]

Not only is the mystical experience amenable to a staggering variety of religious interpretations, ranging from the non-dualism of Sankara to the theism of most Roman Catholic mystics, but it is also possible to cite parallels to the experience in totally secular contexts. Often the descriptions by the artist of the self-transcending ecstasy of the creative act, the rhapsodic accounts by the lover of the bliss found in sexual union, and the reports by drug experimenters of the incomparable "highs" attained can scarcely be distinguished from phenomenological depictions of the mystic state.

Some mystics show a definite preference for "ontological" language, such as "Being" and the "absolute." For them, "the mystical state does not involve having mental images or perceptions . . . and so there is nothing about it to describe."[3] Hence, the more empty and abstract a given expression, the more adequately does it harmonize with and represent the mystical state.

The experience of the Real or Being creates a hunger after total realization, the unification and organization of all values and experiences in such a way that the transitory or "unreal" is discarded, while the permanent, valuable, and real is actualized.[4] In the words of the familiar Hindu prayer:

> Lead me from the unreal to the real;
> Lead me from darkness into light;
> Lead me from the mortal to the immortal.[5]

Like numinous experience, the mystical state discloses an ultimate reality that transcends the mundane world and ordinary experience in dignity and power. However, in most instances the mystic does not encounter this power as a presence offering communion and fellowship. For the mystic, hallowedness is the sense of realization that attends the detachment of the self from the ephemeral and its attachment to the Real. Both the mystic and the worshiper find themselves confronted by actual and potential hallowedness, a sense of harmony between given actions or programs of actions and the Real. But mystical morality does not arise from responses to the demands made by a personal other, but rather from the acceptance of that discipline or spiritual training that enables the individual to discriminate between the Real and the phenomenal so that one's true self may actualize its essential reality or union with the Real. In the words of one observer, "In mysticism there is the passionate desire to penetrate into the very core of reality and to live with it, in it, or even to identify one's self with it in inner sympathy and empathy."[6] The ethical life of numinous religion is fueled by guilt. The morality of mysticism is a conscious striving after wholeness, the deliberate overcoming of unreal separations and distinctions.

In some cultures, ultimate being is identified with God; consequently, mystics in these cultures will perceive God as the inner essence of all natural objects, producing a type of experience that tends toward panentheism or pantheism. In other cultures, the concept of God will not enter into the interpretation of the experience at all. As Alan W. Watts remarked: "The rift between God and nature would vanish if we knew how to experience nature, because what keeps them apart is not a difference of substance but a split in the mind."[7] In a lovely poem, India's Rabindranath Tagore ecstatically explains:

> The same stream of life that runs through my veins night and day runs through the world and dances in rhythmic measures.
>
> It is the same life that shoots enjoy through the dust of the earth in numberless blades of grass and breaks into tumultuous waves of leaves and flowers.
>
> It is the same life that is rocked in the ocean—cradle of birth and of death, and in flow.
>
> I feel my limbs are made glorious by the touch of this world of life. And my pride is from the life-throb of ages dancing in my blood this moment.

In words that are unique to Hindu thought, Tagore speaks of a forgotten separation:

> How often, great Earth, have I felt my being yearn to flow over you, sharing in the happiness of each green blade that rises its signal banner in answer to the beckoning blue of the sky!
>
> I feel as if I have belonged to you ages before I was born. . . .
>
> When, in the evening, the cattle return to their folds, raising dust from the meadow paths, as the moon rises higher than the slope ascending from the village huts, I feel sad as for some great separation that happened in the first morning of existence.[8]

The extrovertive mystic, like Tagore, looks out through the world of experience and there finds the One. But the introvertive mystic turns inward to discover the One at the core of the self, at the very center of human personality.

Introvertive mysticism calls for the "total suppression of the whole empirical content of consciousness,"[9] the pursuit of techniques through which the ordinary sensory-intellectual consciousness disappears so that it may be replaced by an entirely new kind of awareness.

Obviously we cannot stop our ordinary sensory-intellectual processes by willing their cessation. The usual technique employed by mystics is to focus the mind and the senses elsewhere, through some form of meditation—through breathing exercises or the constant recitation of a prayer or short formula of words over and over again until the words lose all meaning. As Stace notes, it is immaterial whether the formula repeated is a psalm, a part of the Lord's Prayer, or the mystic's own name. What is important is that there is a single point of concentration, not what this point is—"whether it be one's breathing, or the sound of one's own name, or one's navel, or anything else, provided only it serves to shut off all other mental content."[10] But, maintains Stace, whatever technique the mystic chooses, the result is the same. By exhausting or paralyzing normal attention and thought, the mystic prepares himself or herself for the moments of consciousness that are ineffable and indescribable.

Consciously or, more likely, unconsciously, those who aspire to the mystical vision bring to the task an attitude of self-surrender, a "feeling of spiritlessness," that leads at last "to the exhaustion of the spirit."[11] The individual surrenders not only his or her self-consciousness, but also the socially derived myths that are the basis of daily existence. In their quest for the mystical state of union with the Real, mystics regress to levels of consciousness and feelings that are prior to the illusions and myths that habitually motivate them as members of society. Hence, mysticism is essentially asocial, individualistic, and private. At the same time, it would be inappropriate to term it fundamentally self-centered. Mystics see themselves as those who have awakened while society, absorbed in what is useless, continues to slumber.

This awakening leads not to the discovery of one's true being but to its loss. True mysticism is not concerned with the enhancement of the individual personality but with its abnegation. It does not regard other persons or nature as mirrors. It wants to turn them into windows through which the divine light streams in. By stripping away the accumulated layers of unreality, the true self is brought to the surface so that it may return to the all-encompassing One, so that the isolated drop of rain may merge with the primordial sea.

New Age and Religious Experience

How does New Age fit into all this? The Aquarian consciousness is restless, symbol-filled, and interpretation-hungry. It cannot be reduced to any of the three types of religious experience, and yet it ransacks all of them in its search for meaning. For New Age, mysticism and naturism are sources of profound confirmation; yet, the numinous is scarcely excluded. However, in its quest for compatible symbol-pictures, rituals, and explanations, New Age, for the most part, bypasses the major forms of Christian theology.

New Age finds little in mainline Protestantism, for the major denominational churches have turned a good deal of their attention away from religious states to social and ethical concerns. The mainstream reacts to all forms of ecstatic religious experience as though they are aberrant. Fundamentalism arises in the life of the individual with crisis conversion, but its attention quickly turns to purity of doctrine and avoidance of vice. Its everyday God looks suspiciously like the projection on the heavens of the superego of a guilty person.

Catholicism lost much of the mystery of its rituals when it translated them from Latin into inelegant, unpoetic vernacular versions. Without mystery, there is insufficient stimulation of the myth-creating imagination. Awe and wonder are watered down. Virtually only the Pentecostals and the

neo-pentecostals of the charismatic movement remain
focused on numinous experience.

Where mainline Christianity prevails, New Age flourishes.
It supplies the ecstatic element without which religion
stagnates, becoming either respectable and irrelevant or
activistic and divisive. Where fundamentalism flourishes,
New Age becomes an option for the marginalized—ethnic
minorities, the divorced, unwed mothers, gays and lesbians,
and others who feel excluded and ostracized. Here New Age
becomes a coalition of those rejected by and rejecting of
fundamentalism. Where charismatic Christianity is strong,
New Age endures the fierce attacks of Pentecostal preachers
and teachers but ignores them and slowly blends right in. The
overlapping and often indistinguishable audiences of New
Age and charismatic Christianity drift from prophet to sage
to seer to teacher to guru, wondering whose magic really
ensures health, wealth, and protection from evil.

The New Agers I have interviewed in recent years fall into
four broad classifications: (1) those who were reared in the
church but found it irrelevant; (2) those who were never
exposed to Christianity other than in the loose, popular, "civil
religion" manifestations and who find the church irrelevant;
(3) those who looked to the church for legitimate ways of
routinizing their intimations of eternity, but were disappointed by what they found or rejected because they were
different; and (4) those who through transforming personal
experiences and resultant insights have come to see the
church as the target and the enemy.

Every type of religious experience is found in New Age.
For the most part, New Agers cannot find the holy in the
church or in any of its versions of what is real and important.
Yet, followers of the New Age are burned and singed by the
presence of the holy in their lives. It is not that they are
desperate, as many observers maintain, as much as they are
overwhelmed. There is something out there and in here, a
power that disrupts, attracts, and frightens. There is a lure of

symbol-pictures and feeling-states. There is a desire to
return—but to whom or to what? There are moments of bliss
and beatitude as well as depths of despair and aloneness.
While the church runs the sands of the hourglass through its
filters of orthodoxy and orthopraxy (right opinion and right
practice), grains of living truth explode and burn with
incandescence throughout the air. For New Agers the church
has no monopoly on the truth. Worse still, the sands that the
church filters are, for the devotees of the New Age, dead ash,
glowing with not even the embers of the Real.

So the New Agers turn to other versions of the heavens
(UFOs, spiritual masters from outer space, disincarnate
beings on other astral planes, hidden sages in Tibetan
mountain caves, or dolphins from the depths of the seas).
They cannot believe in the God whom they think deserted the
human race after dictating the New Testament (or, to be
more personal about it, the God who was present to them
when they were children and young adults, but who has had
nothing to say to them since then). So they look for gods who
are available, at hand, and unavoidably present. Pentecostalism is an expression of the same discomfort with a God who
nodded off two thousand years ago. And a remarkable
number of seekers pass back and forth between the
charismatic movement and the channelers.[12]

In New Age, the religious experience of nature and the
quest to return to the One are prominent—although I cannot
say that they predominate. For some, the encounter with
awesome, fascinating, and terrifying mysteries is at the center
of the individual's experience. Some articulations and
routinizations are purer than others. Some are hopelessly
complex admixtures of elements: mysticism, naturism,
magic, and bunk.

Behind guilt-fueled, right-hand New Age, it is not hard to
see the alluring dance of Mother Earth as well as impulses
arising from extrovertive mysticism. A nature mystic, such as
Rabindranath Tagore, would have understood their ecologi-

cal concerns, their ethics, and their quest for a culture, but he would have wondered why they are so afraid of the agony and ecstasy of love.

Behind the left-hand Aquarian faddism of the gurus, spirit guides, and healers, it is impossible to ignore God as the divine-demonic, as naked power that is neither good nor evil, yet is both. From such a cauldron comes all that is creative and destructive, healing and killing. It is a frightening brew, and there are none who can consume it without themselves being consumed.

When I was a young adult adrift in the world of evangelical Christianity, I was amazed by how complex that realm was. Among my acquaintances I numbered the naive and the sophisticated. I knew those whose spiritual quest was personal/experiential and those who had inherited their religion from their parents. I saw instances of remarkable, miraculous conversion, and I also witnessed the psychological manipulation of subjects by gospel hucksters. I personally experienced beneficial, benign, and malignant manifestations of revivalism. Or should I say that I experienced manifestations of revivalism that were, at various times and under various circumstances, beneficial, benign, or malignant to me?

The same dichotomies characterize manifestations of the New Age. I have met the naive and the sophisticated, the credulous and the clever. I have interviewed those who pursue everything and anything as long as it is new and different, who assume and discard identities like snakes shedding skins. I have encountered those who will believe anything and those who will keep selling nostrums as long as there are credulous buyers. I have run into con artists and sociopaths whom I wish I had never known. I know those who identify with New Age because they have read a book, attended a lecture, or memorized an aphorism ("What goes around comes around"; "There are no absolutes"; "What you believe is what you receive"; and so on).

But in more forms of New Age than I am able to count, I have also met spiritual pioneers and adventurers, lovers of the divine, friends of the constant companion, worshipers, healers, dreamers, mystics, and teachers. To be fair, I would note that I have also stumbled over them in fundamentalism, in liberal Protestantism, in Catholicism, in charismatic Christianity, in Judaism, in Hinduism, in Buddhism, in Islam, and in places of irreligion, skepticism, and doubt.

There are forms of New Age that are beneficial, forms that are benign, and forms that are malignant. And once again I confess that I have experienced manifestations of New Age that were, at various times and under various circumstances, beneficial, benign, or malignant to me.

The tradition to which I have been called says that human beings are made in the image of God and that we are only a little less than the angels. Perhaps we have not taken that seriously enough while the nature worshipers, the new mystics, the channelers, and the healers have. But do they know what sorcerer they apprentice? Can they get the genie back in the bottle? Do they know that the whirlwinds with which they play conceal God?

CHAPTER NINE

Ufos, Health, and Death

The Serpent [addressing Adam and Eve]: You see things; and you say, "Why?" But I dream things that never were; and I say, "Why not?"
—George Bernard Shaw,
Back to Methuselah, Part 1, Act I.

The prisoner who lost faith in the future—his future—was doomed. With his loss of belief in the future, he also lost his spiritual hold; he let himself decline and became subject to mental and physical decay. . . . Those who know how close the connection is between the state of a man—his courage and hope, or lack of them—and the state of immunity of his body will understand that the sudden loss of hope and courage can have a deadly effect. The ultimate cause of my friend's death was . . . [that] he was severely disappointed.
—Viktor E. Frankl, "Experiences in a Concentration Camp."

Meaning from Outer Space

Carl is a UFO abductee. He did not know it until he was hypnotized. While in a trance, he remembered being awakened by a bright light and a rumbling sound. His room was cold and filled with a cloud of mist. Suddenly a pair of

155

short, hairless creatures wearing shiny silver suits appeared. Without ever speaking a word, they communicated to him that he was in no danger. Then one pointed some sort of hand-held instrument at him, and he was levitated into a shaft of light that carried him right through the ceiling of his room and the roof of his house into a hovering flying saucer.

He was strapped to a shiny examination table and probed with strange instruments. Although he felt no pain, long hypodermic needles were thrust into his stomach, his chest, his head, and his scrotum. During the examination, he passed out.

When he awoke again, he was in his bed, feeling at peace with himself and the world in a way that he had never known before.

During subsequent hypnosis sessions, he recalled that there had not been a single visit to the UFO but several over a period of nearly twenty years. The visitors had told him that they were using his sperm to create a race of superior human beings who would be capable of withstanding thermonuclear war. These new beings would also be wiser, more caring, and more scientifically advanced than present earth creatures. "We seeded your planet thousand of years ago with your ancestors, but things did not work out as we hoped. So now we will try again," the extraterrestrials informed him.

The space beings instructed Carl to leave his stress-laden job and find a simpler existence in the country. He had done as they instructed. Carl became a much more contented, peaceful human being than he had been a few years earlier. And the debilitating spinal deterioration that had afflicted him since he was a child has completely disappeared.

Henry is another UFO abductee. He, too, learned of his "hidden memories" during a psychology experiment at the state university. He and several classmates, who had neither previous UFO experience nor interest in the subject, were hypnotized and told to imagine being taken aboard a spacecraft. In the words of one observer: "The students produced fantasy journeys remarkably similar in detail and chronology to 'authentic' abduction accounts."[1]

Henry dismisses his "memories" as delusions that drifted from his subconscious to his conscious mind and remained there as posthypnotic "pseudo-memories." He notes no change in his behavior, feelings, or attitudes as a result of his "fantasies."

For Carl, his abduction by space beings was a religious experience, one which gave his life meaning and direction. For Henry, his experience with the aliens and the spacecraft was a somewhat interesting fantasy, of no lasting significance.

Carl has traveled the country speaking to groups gathered at local motels. He is a vibrant, convincing advocate of the position that humankind has friends out there and that they are trying to help us help ourselves.

Six years ago, Carl disappeared. Food was cooking on the stove; his clothes were in the closet; his bed was unmade. His parents were alarmed and contacted the police. Suspecting that he had wandered off with a UFO sect (of which there are several), the police referred the parents to me. For five years, there was not a clue. It was as though the great saucer from the Orion Nebulae had returned for Carl as he had predicted. As the months passed, similar reports reached me from various parts of California, Nevada, and Idaho. About forty UFO contactees like Carl were missing. And then the communications with families began. First a postcard was received by one family from their missing son, saying, "I am O.K. Call off the dogs!" Then two of the contactees surfaced in a ghost town in Arizona. One or two at a time, the missing persons returned to their families.

Carl told me that he and the others had spent the time camping together in a secluded part of Montana, waiting for the promised spacecraft. When it did not come, they were told by "mental radio" to disperse, remain hidden, and wait for further instructions. Carl and two of the others had worked under assumed names as gold miners in northern

California. Finally, he began to worry about what his aged parents might be thinking, and he decided to go home. I asked about his health. "You mean, my spine?" he replied, then he laughed and singsonged, "My spine is fine." About a year ago, the extraterrestrials introduced Carl to a tiny creature, half human and half extraterrestrial—his own son.

The mother of another missing contactee phoned me and asked me to stop looking for her son. Her story was that the group had actually been taken aboard the UFO in Montana, that they had been "trained" for a special mission of rearing the hybrid space children, and that they and the star children had scattered throughout the world.

It is easy to dismiss Carl's experiences as delusions. Perhaps he unknowingly created them out of the shared cultural archetypes that have floated around in movies, the tabloids, and popular books since World War II. Perhaps they are expression of his fears and frustrations. Maybe under hypnosis he actually relived his own birth trauma. His descriptions of the aliens, with their hairless bodies, large heads, and huge eyes, sound suspiciously like embryos. The probing and testing aboard the sterile, silver spacecraft suggests postnatal examination in a modern hospital.[2] But whatever really happened, the fact remains that Carl is a different person today from whom he was before his experiences with the extraterrestrials.

A friend of mine spent several years and many thousands of dollars attempting to relive his past lives so that he could free himself of the traumas preventing him from succeeding in his present existence. Were his recollections pseudo-memories? Now that he is thoroughly disillusioned with the past life regressionist who guided him in his quest, he would say that they were and that the therapist took advantage of his credulity by manipulating his past lives in order to make him dependent. My friend relates: "The therapist kept 'remind-ing' me of more and more traumas that had to be worked out. The more sessions I paid for, the more I needed. Pretty soon my whole life was regression. I spent so much time worrying about past lives that I didn't have time to live this one. And the therapist kept telling me that my wife and friends were against me in this life just as they had been in my previous lives. So I stopped speaking to them. Soon I had no one to talk to other than my therapist. I can't believe how miserable I let myself become." My friend recalls the pain of those days, but I remember the zest, enthusiasm, and *joie de vivre* he evidenced during his therapy. Why has he forgotten?

Sociologist David Swift has observed:

> UFO cults are like a religion, offering comfort and hope to people who are struggling with basic problems of modern life. On the one hand, science and education have undermined our faith in a benevolent God who cares about us. On the other hand, science and education have not provided answers to questions about our origins and goals.
>
> Into this void have stepped the saucer sects, offering us the reassuring belief that benevolent beings from outer space will take care of us, solve our problems, and offer us unimaginable joys.
>
> . . . The UFO, more than any of its competitors, highlights the inadequacies of science, the armed forces, and government. These are among the most powerful institutions in our society yet they are unable to deal with UFOs. . . . No other symbol has so silently but effectively undermined the credibility of our leading institutions . . . the underlying message is so clear that it hardly needs to be verbalized: the creators of this awesome object have fantastic knowledge and power, and this knowledge and power might help you.[3]

So the UFOs show us up for the cosmic bunglers we really are. Although decades of investigation have not yielded one single shred of unambiguous, undeniable physical evidence of their existence, they are still out there in the skies and still firmly anchored in our psyches—intriguing, annoying, frightening, and fascinating us, just like the gods of old. Yet, they forever elude and frustrate us. Science, education, traditional religion, the armed forces, psychology, popular movements, the government, and industry cannot unravel their mystery. Neither can silver-haired, well read, and expert-supported Phil Donahue ("I never go anywhere without a psychologist") nor insightful, probing, and common-sensible Oprah Winfrey.

Note the pattern, for it runs through most New Age manifestations: Individuals feel bereft of power, meaning, and purpose. Traditional institutions and accustomed beliefs and mores seem inadequate and boring. Suddenly there arises on the horizon or within one's consciousness or in one's dreams or in the presence of a stranger or in the words of an arcane text an answer, the answer, the only possible answer.

The Holistic Survivalists

Closer to home, there are more immediate frustrations and fears that rob us of sleep. They deal with survival rather than meaning. We are afraid of the food we eat and the water we drink, afraid of the timesaving microwave ovens in our kitchens, afraid of sugar substitutes in our diet beverages, afraid of the insulation in our walls, afraid of the sun that tans our skin, afraid of alcohol and tobacco, afraid of the power plant a few miles away and the power lines over our heads. Every one of these can cause cancer. Life in the late twentieth century has been revealed to be carcinogenic. The crib in every maternity ward should bear a warning label: "The Surgeon General has determined that life is hazardous to your health."

Just as the UFOs provide a sense of meaning, so also the practitioners of holistic health offer a chance of survival in the face of the myriad threats of lingering death. The concept of psychosomatic illness is nothing new. The realization that some dysfunctions of the body have their origin in the mind and disappear when the underlying emotional causes are repaired is widely recognized. It does not strike us at all

surprising when hysterical symptoms or neurotic manifestations are overcome by love, faith, self-understanding,
voodoo, or a placebo. "It was all in his (or her) head anyway,"
we rationalize.

But recently the power of inner attitudes over such obvious
and undeniable physical conditions as cancer and AIDS have
received significant attention. Consider the following passage from *Love, Medicine and Miracles: Lessons Learned About
Self-Healing from a Surgeon's Experience* by Bernie S. Siegel,
M.D.:

> I always try to get patients to see standard medical
> treatments—such as radiation, chemotherapy, and surgery—
> as energy that can heal them. They buy time during which I
> can help the patient find the will to live, change, and heal.
> Many of the disagreements over the worth of alternate
> therapies arise because some people heal themselves no
> matter what external aids they choose, as long as they have
> hope and some control over the therapy. I support them as
> long as a patient has chosen them with a positive conviction,
> not out of fear. . . .
>
> I try to get patients to understand that the body heals, not
> the therapy. All healing is scientific. At a recent conference,
> someone told me he knew of someone on a macrobiotic diet,
> someone else on a diet exactly the opposite, and a third person
> on chemotherapy and radiation. All three got well, and this
> person couldn't understand how the body could accomplish
> this or how the treatments made any sense. But the body can
> utilize any form of energy for healing—even Krebiozen or
> plain water—as long as the patient believes in it.
>
> Let's say I recommend eating three peanut butter sand-
> wiches a day to cure cancer. Some people would get well and
> claim it was the peanut butter that did it. Then even more
> people would have hope, eat peanut butter, and get better,
> too. But we know it's not the peanut butter. It's their hope and
> the changes they produce in their lives while they're on the
> new therapy.

> The most important thing is to pick a therapy you believe in
> and proceed with a positive attitude.[4]

Siegel recognizes that fear, apprehension, and panic
interfere with every form of treatment and that confidence,
trust, and joy allow the body to heal itself. So far so good. But
popular New Age thinking goes much farther. Writers like
Louise Hay insist that our thoughts cause our existence, that
we think ourselves sick, and that physical illnesses can be
overcome by deliberately changing our thought patterns. In
her book *Heal Your Body: The Mental Causes for Physical Illness
and the Metaphysical Way to Overcome Them*, she offers a list of
physical ailments and their associated mental attitudes,
together with positive affirmations to overcome them. For
example, Hay maintains that abscesses are caused by
"fermenting thoughts over hurts, slights, revenge." The
prescribed affirmation: "I allow my thoughts to be free. The
past is over. I am at peace." The probable cause of AIDS is
"denial of the self. Sexual guilt. A strong belief in not being
'good enough.' " The recommended affirmations: "I am a
Divine, magnificent expression of life. I rejoice in my
sexuality. I rejoice in all that I am. I love myself."[5]

With Hay, we have drifted from the theory that joy
unblocks the obstacles to healing to the New Thought/New
Age position that we make our own reality, that the
circumstances of our daily existence do not create us, but that
we create them. We have gone beyond the healing of disease
to the transformation of the total person. Perhaps we have
gone from faith to magic.

As a counselor, I know that for clients to realize that they
are responsible for their lives, that they are not the automatic,
irremediable outcome of some fixed lottery, is a powerful
and liberating insight. If and when it is internalized, the
awareness that the individual is not a victim, that the past does
not have absolute power over the present, that limitations can
be transcended, sweeps away in an instant decades of

frustration and depression. I also have seen that without a supporting structure of daily routine and interpersonal support, such insights have the shelf life of ripe bananas.

But to go farther and to attempt to ascribe to every physical ailment a specific attitude that can be overcome by the repeated daily enunciation of a few sentences boggles the mind. To be fair to Hay, when I look closely at the table of probable causes and New Thought cures, when I read between the lines, I do not find several diseases with an appropriate cure for each, but a single malaise and a single prescription. In sum, there is only one problem—not loving oneself—and one solution—loving oneself. All the affirmations say one and the same thing: I am an expression of the divine life. I am worthy. I choose to accept and enjoy myself. Meditating on such sentiments, repeating them again and again, and offering them to God in prayer can change attitudes, patterns of behavior, and circumstances. I know that. But can they eradicate illness and suffering?

Consider India, the home of the spiritual perspectives so valued by New Age thinkers. It was not positive thinking or meditation or chanting that conquered typhoid, cholera, and small pox. To the extent that such scourges have been eliminated at all, it has not been through India's centuries-old pursuit of transcendent reality, but through such rational approaches as sanitary engineering and vaccination.

Not all New Age holistic healers are as concerned with ideas and attitudes as Hay. "Body work" approaches the causes of physical distress not in the mind, but directly in the body. Through a variety of techniques ranging from acupuncture to deep massage, body workers locate stresses, or "energy blockages," in the muscles and tissues and seek to release them. Some practitioners combine body work with talking therapy, exercise, mud baths, colonics, special diets, meditation, visualization, herbal therapy, color therapy, and/or devotion to a particular guru. Others show little concern for anything other than the alleviation of bodily discomfort. What most body workers have in common is the conviction that emotions are as much physical sensations as ideas and that as such they should be worked out where they are actually experienced.

In both the "change your ideas in order to change your life" form and the multiplicity of body work approaches, the New Age analysis of pain and suffering almost gives the individual too much responsibility. Metaphysical affirmationists, in particular, leave us with more questions than answers. A friend of mine lost a child to sudden crib death. Did that child not love himself enough? Another friend fought valiantly and courageously to overcome a congenital heart defect. His life was full and fruitful. His faith in God was inspiring. He was a cause of joy to hundreds. Yet, he died in his forties. Was there some lack of self-love here? On the contrary, he loved and savored every moment of his life with an ardor few of us possess or could sustain.

New Age Approaches to AIDS

Consider New Age approaches to AIDS. The editors of *Psychoimmunity and the Healing Process: A Holistic Approach to Immunity and AIDS* state:

> We believe that the AIDS virus particularly strikes individuals and groups who have been isolated by the dominant culture—culturally isolated minorities who are forced to express their emotional, physical, and spiritual nature apart from the community at large. . . . Societal isolation places unusually heightened degrees of stress upon the individual and collective mind, body, and spirit of its outcasts. It is this isolation, often internalized as self-hatred or lack of self-acceptance, which allows the AIDS virus to begin to incubate once it has entered the system. . . .
>
> It is no coincidence that the rise of AIDS has to a large extent coincided with the recent upsurge of right-wing political and religious repression of gays.[6]

Are we to understand that highly visible and vocal gay-bashers have caused AIDS by undermining the tolerance of the community toward homosexual life-styles? That their negativity so powerfully influences gays and Haitians that the immune systems of these "despised minorities" simply collapsed? This is exactly what the authors of the book maintain.

How then do we treat the victims of the disease? Is it accurate to call them "victims," or should we say "those who as the result of self-loathing forced on them by right-wingers and fundamentalists have chosen to allow themselves to contract the disease"? In *AIDS: A Positive Approach*, Louise Hay offers a program of self-affirmation, nutrition, and medical support to overcome the illness. I have seen her on talk shows with clients who claim to have been cured by her counseling, their own transformed self-images, and the support of their fellow AIDS sufferers. What does the medical community have to say about these claims? Not a word. Does Louise Hay "cure" AIDS? Is it all so simple? Can a few well chosen sentences repeated daily stop the AIDS scourge? Apparently not. Religion writer Don Lattin reports the following dialogue:

> Jim took the cordless microphone and turned toward Louise Hay, who sat cross-legged on a table before a small auditorium overflowing with 350 people, most of them with AIDS-related illnesses.
>
> "Why do some people who work so hard with your books and tapes still get sick and pass on?" he asked.
>
> Hay . . . paused before answering.
>
> "I wish I knew the answer," said Hay. . . . "With most diseases, you can make incredible change with your mental work, but we haven't found the answer yet," she said. "Sometimes the longer AIDS goes on, the less I feel I know about it."[7]

When will the terrible AIDS plague disappear? When will a

cure be found? Soli, a Spirit Entity who speaks through the Reverend Neville Row, provides one answer:

> When it is no longer necessary to have a disease such as AIDS upon the Earth plane, when no one needs the experience anymore, then someone from the Spirit side may very well pass the idea to someone on the Earth plane and a so-called "cure" will come forward. . . . Cures come when the disease is no longer necessary. There are no accidents. As long as there are those who need to have the experience of leaving the Earth by AIDS . . . it will stay upon the Earth plane. . . .
>
> As more and more individuals go within and discover their own inner guidance, work on themselves, take responsibility for their own lives, then less and less is their need for what some would see as catastrophe or tragedy . . . when there is no further need for those experiences, then there will be no further need for that illness or experience to be manifest and it will go away.[8]

I have deliberately constructed this bridge of materials, taking us from Siegel's "what you believe can allow your body to heal itself" to the Spirit Soli's claim that when we no longer need the experience of an illness, it will go away, in order to express how New Age is at once extremely comforting and extremely disquieting. In its attitude toward cancer and AIDS, it offers hope, returns the responsibility for the problem directly to the sufferer, and heads for higher planes of metaphysical reality. Does it not sound suspiciously like the popular Christian way of dealing with evil? The world in which we live is screwed up. Somehow we did it. At some time in the future, God will straighten it out. In the meantime, those who believe can be healed of their infirmities, forgiven of their sins, and enjoy a foretaste of eternal life in the fellowship of the saints and the communion of the Spirit. Like the Christian explication, does it not all depend on faith, on what meaning we give to our experiences, on the frame of reference we accept, on the powerful affective states that now and then capriciously break through and realign our inner compasses?

Do not the New Age as well as the Christian accounts of what is wrong and what we should do about it leave us wondering why some are healed and some are left to die? Jennifer, a beautiful young socialite from San Francisco, went forward at a healing service in an independent charismatic church and accepted a healing of her coughing spells, praising and thanking Jesus. Within a year, she was dead of lung cancer. The healing evangelist says that the socialite's faith became weak and, hence, Jennifer forfeited her healing. Yet, when the healer's own husband developed prostate cancer, he underwent surgery and chemotherapy. Why was she unable to heal him?

Can faith be quantified? Are there degrees of faiths? Quantities of faith? Kinds of faith?

Why are only some of Louise Hay's counselees cured of AIDS? Do some repeat the affirmations more than others? Do some believe them more fervently? What determines why some believe and some do not? Is any choice involved? Do some individuals naturally have a greater will to believe than others?

After nearly thirty years of attending to the claims of faith healers, metaphysical healers, body workers, hypnotherapists, gurus, Jesus impersonators, and alleged incarnations of God, I have only one answer: *Sometimes the magic works, and sometimes it doesn't.*

The Wandering Monks

One of the most unusual New Age publications, *Monk*, details the wanderings of two scrawny men (Michael Lane and James Marshall Crotty) with their pet cats and a Macintosh computer in their 1972 Ford van. Although *Monk* is mostly a satire influenced by *The National Lampoon*, it contains touching vignettes of "artists" and "monks" met on "the path of peace" by "the Monks" (Lane and Crotty). Particularly moving is the story of Stephan Frease, former Beverly Hills fitness instructor, who is now an artist based in Aspen, Colorado. As *Monk* relates:

> While Stephan knows the peaks of fame, fitness and laughter, he also knows the depths of despair. He became known as "the guru of sweat" before life in the L.A. fast lane and his son's battle with bone cancer caused him to pack his gym bag and head for the Rockies. Stephan's son Devon was a tennis star, a straight A student and a very close friend of his father. "We were like romantic lovers," Stephan recalls. For five years Stephan tried everything from crystals to Macrobiotics to help heal his son, but at 18 Devon left his body.[9]

Writing in his diary during his son's illness, Stephan declared:

> **Children's Hospital.** Old souls wrapped in children's bodies. Scores of wise old men and women peering out from the clear-sky eyes of angels. . . .
>
> The broadness of his smile matching the broadness of our hope. I am in love with life! My son will live. He will play tennis with me again, and go to the movies, and have a girlfriend!
>
> In the mountains. Alone with note pad, a cup of tea, a breeze that might be described as a single splash of pastel watercolor across a page. Where will I find my dear son Devon when he is gone? Will he smile at me from across the heavens? Will the wind echo his voice, or a flower reflect his face? Where will he be? How will I live without him? I may have come beyond the asking of "why," but not beyond the asking of "how?" In a way I envy him. He will be alright. . . .

And if all else fails, if the crystals and the macrobiotic diets prove ineffectual, if my loved one dies or I am dying, there is the message that death is not the end of the story. On their travels, the Monks met Ly Le, a Vietnamese woman in her late thirties. Raised amid the carnage of war, Ly Le was no stranger to the threat of death. The Monks observe:

> As Le grew, she became acquainted with a world animated by spirits or what she calls "ghosts." A magical world where past and present merged, where death became a part of life. When a member of her family died their body was placed in the center of the house where for three days they honored the spirit. Coins were placed in the eyes and small vessels of rice, water and incense were placed nearby. From here she learned to talk to the dead, to honor them, to keep the communication flowing. Death did not mean an end to life but only a change of form in which life existed.[10]

Le married an American serviceman and settled in America. Her reverence for spirits was ridiculed by her husband and her new family. At times she felt that she was going insane. The Monks poignantly describe her plight:

> It was later, after the birth of several sons, that her husband tragically died, and she was once again confronted with a new challenge, that of being a single mother with a family to support. The passing of her husband was a confusing time. She wanted to honor his body and spirit in the traditions of her past, but his family refused her such "barbaric" customs. And her tender heart melted as she conformed to our "civilized" rituals around death. A week after his death she recounts the call from acquaintances who wanted to take her out for pizza. She had never heard of pizza and thought that this might be the ceremony for releasing his spirit. Throughout the evening she kept looking for clues for the anticipated ritual. . . . But her hopes turned to grief when, after being dropped off at her home, she realized she had merely been taken out to dinner.[11]

When Le and the Monks shared dinner at her home, she spoke with great tenderness of "her continuing reverence for the world of spirit," of her commitment to serving the poor and the sick in her community, and of sharing her tradition and culture with her friends. The Monks recall:

> She later took [us] . . . up to her private temple where she became like a young girl showing her favorite toys. We knelt before her altar and said a brief prayer, a prayer for opening our eyes to the world of spirit. . . .
>
> Le teaches that the world is sacred. She teaches that every possession, every act is an expression of the divine. Her every word is charged with life and joy. And even now we can see her twinkling Buddha eyes saying yes, unlock your door. Don't be afraid. You and your spirit have arrived.[12]

Hospices and Hope

In recent years, an entire industry has arisen to deal with the needs of the dying. Pioneered by Elisabeth Kübler-Ross, hospices offering specialized services for the terminally ill, grief counseling for survivors, and attitudinal healing for the dying and the bereaved have sprung up in many hundreds of places at once as though in response to a silent signal. What ideology dominates such programs? Many Catholic, traditional mainline, and evangelical Christians have found their vocation in this work. Beth Spring, contributing editor to *Christianity Today,* is concerned that hospice has been infiltrated by New Agers. She writes: "Hospice's roots are often thought to be humanistic, with little regard for a Christian understanding of life and death . . . some hospices may be infected by the New Age movement." And again:

> In its early days, hospice was associated with some questionable trends and ideas, such as Elisabeth Kübler-Ross's spiritualism. Christian hospice workers admit they now face a challenge from the New Age movement. In particular, programs that are expressly nonsectarian may find their staff members influenced

by books and seminars theorizing on out-of-the-body experiences and communication with spirits.[13]

I am aware that literature about the "near death experiences" of patients who have been revived after clinical death is quite popular in New Age circles. Such accounts seem to offer empirical validation for the notion of survival of the human spirit after physical extinction. Elisabeth Kübler-Ross, who has done more than anyone else to popularize the hospice cause, allowed herself, several years ago, to be taken advantage of by individuals using sleight-of-hand tricks to conjure up the "ectoplasmic" forms of the departed. But does this mean that the hospice movement is in danger? In danger of what? Is there some sort of official Christian view of death and dying? Can Christians really interpret the Bible to tell them what exactly happens to the spirit of an individual human at the time of death or five minutes later? Is there an immortal soul that goes to heaven? Or is this just popular, superstitious piety? Where does the undying part of a human being go, and what does it do until the final resurrection?

If the answers to such questions were clear in Christian theology, I would have more sympathy for evangelical attempts to limit New Age influence in the hospice field. As matters stand, such defensiveness sounds paranoid. Once again, New Age makes inroads because it deals directly with real fears and frustrations; and, once again, evangelical Christians react as though hordes of infidels were hammering at the gates.

I am reminded of the reaction of UFO theorist and information scientist Jacques Vallee to attending a New Age exposition not far from where I live.

A Great celebration, in San Francisco. A thousand young people, the nucleus of everything psychic and countercultural in Northern California, have gathered in a large auditorium. There are booths selling health food, cosmic advice, tantric yoga courses, and consciousness training. A colorful crowd pulsates through the aisles and fills the seminar rooms. The One World Family Commune of Berkeley runs a restaurant. It is directed by Allan the Messiah, wearing a impeccable red uniform and advertising the Everlasting Gospel revealed to him by the saucers. His information indicates that the earth is in fact hollow, with the saucer people inside.[14]

There is a strange urge in my mind: I would like to stop behaving as a rat pressing levers—even if I have to go hungry for a while. I would like to step outside the conditioning maze and see what makes it tick. I wonder what I would find. Perhaps a superhuman monstrosity the very contemplation of which would make a man insane? Perhaps a solemn gathering of wise men? Or the maddening simplicity of unattended clockwork?[15]

Make fun of New Age. Belittle New Age. Commercialize New Age. Trivialize New Age. Shake a fist at New Age. Push an open Bible in its face. And it persists. Why? The ultimate success of a social movement does not depend on the number of its recruits, the sophistication of its leadership, the educational attainments of its membership, the state of its finances, or the prestige with which it is regarded by the media. It depends, rather, on the responsiveness of the movement to the needs of large numbers of people; on its ability to articulate the hurts, wants, and aspirations of those without voice in a given society; and, above all, on the vision it conveys of a hopeful future—a future attainable by individuals through the group, and only through the group.

Seventy years ago, William Sadler, a prominent physiologist, wrote:

We are now passing through a period of popular reaction against the scientific materialism of the last century. The common people are awakening to the fact that the mental state has much to do with bodily health and disease. The bookmakers, in their efforts to satisfy the universal demand for teaching on various phases of mental healing, have flooded us with literature, much of which is premature, unscientific, incomplete, and highly disastrous in its misleading influence upon the popular mind and morals.[16]

Several decades later, we are up to our eyeballs in channeled messages, alternative therapies, telegrams from outer space, horoscopes, crystals, and soothsayers. Would Dr. Sadler still find our musings premature, unscientific, incomplete, and mentally and morally destructive? Or would he acknowledge that humankind must dream on through symbols and myths and intuitions and hunches; that men and women, individually and collectively, must seek—in ways fraught with peril, self-contradiction, and ambiguity—to discover their own power and their own limitations?

CHAPTER TEN

New Age Meets the Gospel

There are two ways of thinking "I am God." If you think, "I here, in my physical presence and in my temporal character, am God," then you are mad and have short-circuited the experience. You are God, not in your ego, but in your deepest being, where you are at one with the nondual transcendent.

—Joseph Campbell, *The Power of Myth*

New Age Hero

I read a book recently about a man who
as a child had his own private astrologers,
was visited by beings from a higher plane,
lived in an exotic foreign land,
conversed with leading spiritual teachers,
as an adult he became
a healer,
a channeler,
a magician,
a revealer of the wisdom of another plane,
a supplier of strange, wondrous foods,
a contactee of extraterrestrial beings,
an associate of long-dead spiritual teachers,

an abductee who went up in the sky and never was seen again.

The book is the New Testament.

For New Age, Jesus of Nazareth is not Lord and Savior but a truly human being with all the powers intrinsic to authentic human nature. He is the Son of Man, the example that any human being can follow. What he is, we can be. Did he not promise his disciples that they could work even greater wonders than he had worked (John 14:12)? In the words of Irenaeus of Lyons, an early Christian father: "Our Lord Jesus Christ, the word of God, of his boundless love, became what we are that he might make us what he himself is."[1]

The Aquarian Jesus lives today as the true self incarnate in each one of us and longing to be released as each of us actualizes his or her Christ nature.

When I was twenty-two, I failed the state eye examination required of driver's license applicants. My neighborhood optometrist supplied me with my first pair of glasses. I could see from one side of the street to the other! I could read shop signs and theater marquees! What a wonder!

Jesus the Christ unveils spiritual reality. He opens our eyes whether we are traditionalists or mystics or New Age seekers. His presence in our lives heals and comforts. It also wounds and confuses, for he does not guarantee health, wealth, or security.

Robert A. Raines, director of the Kirkridge retreat center, relates:

> Sometimes we are healed in the presence of one who hears our cries, asks our name and holds us, trembling. A friend writes, "An older woman was desperately ill at the hospital, surrounded by talkative, cheerful, positive thinking relatives who hushed her up every time she tried to say how miserably sick she was. Early Sunday morning I went to see her, and found her thrashing about and moaning. I touched her shoulder, we held hands for awhile; and as she told me how

she felt she became calmer. The thrashing slowed, then
stopped, as did the moaning. When I left she kissed and
blessed me. I can still see the beautiful smile on her face. She
died quietly the next day."[2]

She died. The one who comforted her was served by his
serving. They were both blessed by the living Christ.

As we noted earlier, Christian spiritual awakenings and
New Age manifestations have been inseparably linked for
centuries. Consider the Salem witch hunt, one of the darkest
pages in American history. A group of impressionable girls
experimented with charms and spells, hoping to alleviate the
boredom of their lives, to entertain themselves, and to learn
whom they would marry. Their guide was Tituba, a freed
slave, a black woman brought from Barbados by Samuel
Parris, the pastor of the village church. In the pastor's home
the girls played with these new arts until they were struck by
inexplicable fits. They fell to the ground, their bodies
contorted by convulsions, their mouths babbling unintelligi-
ble noises. When the medical science of the day proved
unable to diagnose their ailment, the theologians were called
in. The divines detected the hand of Satan and began looking
for the witches who had oppressed the children. Instead of
punishing the children for dabbling with magic, they allowed
them to use their psychic abilities to provide "spectral
evidence" against the alleged witches. They believed the girls'
claims that they could see through their special clairvoyant
powers what ordinary mortals could scarcely imagine.

Spells, incantations, folk magic, visions, possession, voodoo
and occult practices imported from another civilization,
trances, witches, astral projections, and psychic gifts in 1692.
The New Age had already sprung up in America!

In the hysteria that followed, twenty innocent lives were
sacrificed. As sanity returned and rationality prevailed, a
strange thing happened. In another Massachusetts congre-
gation, similarly disquieting manifestations occurred—

uncontrollable terror, weeping and moaning, even the suicide of an afflicted townsman. But in 1735, such disturbances were interpreted not as the works of the Devil, but as manifestations of the Holy Spirit. Under the guidance of the local pastor, Jonathan Edwards, the sufferers passed through their terrors and found peace and fulfillment. As Paul Boyer and Stephen Nissenbaum observe: "In short, several hundred people of Northampton had been . . . not bewitched but converted." They argue: "The crucial difference between the two episodes is the interpretation which the adult leadership of each community placed upon physical and emotional states which in themselves were strikingly similar. In Northampton they were viewed in a divine and hopeful light; in Salem Village they were seized upon as sinister and demonic."[3]

In a few years, the Great Awakening would turn the hearts of the faithless and indolent to God. What would have happened in Salem Village if the pastor, the physicians, or the theologians had seen the hand of the Almighty in those strange, unsettling events of 1692?

Who is at work in our midst three hundred years later?

Serious and Humorous

As I conducted the research for this book, I jotted down my thoughts in a notebook headed: "New Age Gospel." My goal was to collect short sayings that could form the basis for discussions that I might conduct (a) with Christians who were interested in New Age or (b) with New Agers who were willing to discuss their attitudes with Christians. These aphorisms listed below represent my viewpoint on the matters explored throughout these pages. Together with the hundreds of forms of religious experience I have encountered in the past forty years, New Age manifestations continually fascinate and exasperate me. My interviews, readings, and other exposures to New Age regularly elicit from me a "Yes, but . . ." reaction. As much as I agree, I reserve the right to differ.

When I first communicated "New Age Gospel" to an audience (at the Coolidge Colloquium in Cambridge, Massachusetts, in June 1988), several of my peers asked me whether I meant the material to be taken seriously or "tongue-in-cheek." The only honest answer is: Yes! "Serious/humorous" is the first of many dichotomies that the observer will have to lay aside in order to appreciate New Age. As Joseph Campbell remarked:

> A key difference between mythology and our Judeo-Christian religion is that the imagery of mythology is rendered with humor. You realize that the image is symbolic of something. You're at a distance from it. But in our religion, everything is prosaic, and very, very serious. You can't fool around with Yahweh.[4]

New Age Gospel

There are more things in heaven and earth than are imagined in your philosophy.

There is a dimension of depth—of wonder and play—which is best appropriated through awe than through reason. However, this does not mean that because something is irrational it is real or important.

There are untapped resources within the self that enable us to create, to heal ourselves, to help others, to envision a better world. There is also a great deal of confusion, pain, and mischief.

Death is not the last word, but no one knows what the last word is.

There are worlds within worlds, worlds within each of us, and worlds beyond worlds.

Body, mind, and spirit are not separate realities. They are distinct, yet inseparable, aspects of the same reality.

Most illness, physical as well as mental, is caused by lack of meaning in one's life. Healing is never complete unless one is restored to the ground of one's being and meaning. To avoid illness, maintain a positive attitude toward life, but don't forget what your mother taught you about cleanliness, proper diet, adequate rest, and not sleeping around.

Most of one's problems are self-induced. Most self-induced problems can be self-resolved, but having a supportive circle helps.

Most of what one regards as good is that with which one is comfortable. Most of what one regards as evil is that with which one is uncomfortable. The known is more comfortable—even when it is painful—than the unknown is, even when it is potentially blissful.

Each individual's personality includes masculine and feminine characteristics. Men are essentially as nurturing and dependent as women, and women as creative and powerful as men. The differences between the sexes are, for the most part, social fictions. Like most social fictions, this one is used by the powerful to justify the exploitation of the powerless. Women can bear children and lactate. Men cannot. Men on the average are somewhat physically stronger than women. Beyond this, there are no essential differences.

The only absolute belief is the belief that all beliefs are relative. One's interpretation of reality is a multi-player, interpersonal Ping-Pong game within a given social context. One has no choice but to play. Those who try not to play are ill treated—labeled insane, bad, deviant, or satanic. One cannot escape the influences of one's social context—no matter where one goes, the Ping-Pong game continues, but one can enlarge the size of the table and thereby gain a new perspective.

No one has a monopoly on the truth. There is no right way and no wrong way.

Truth is the meaning that one creates within and beyond the Ping-Pong game.

No matter what one believes or how one defines reality, heavy objects still fall and a chair left in the way will stub your toe when you get up in the middle of the night and wander to the bathroom for a drink of water.

No objective fact can make life as beautiful as a dream. No dream can fix a broken leg or buy a loaf of bread at the 7-11.

Even psychics own telephones.

Religion is both the reception and the distortion of revelation. There is no such thing as a revealed religion. Even a perfect revelation cannot protect itself from being misinterpreted and distorted by imperfect human beings. The notion that a single interpreter's or a community of interpreters' single interpretation of the divine or of the Bible is final is obscene. It is also understandable.

Knowledge of only one religion is knowledge of none. Just as no one teaches himself or herself how to speak, no person can teach himself or herself how to respond to revelation. A community of faith provides a community of interpretation. The response of and interaction with multiple communities of faith provides a context in which any given community of faith understands itself. However, unless an individual intimately knows/practices/participates within his or her community of faith (either that in which he or she was born or that which he or she has chosen), all communities of faith remain opaque.

God is a figment of our imaginations, and we are the products of God's. God may be found within, but not everything within is of God.

No one escapes.

No one escapes alone.

Someone has to go first.

No one is God except God. It may be that we are all manifestations of God, moments in the life of God, dreams of

God, jokes of God. But for an individual to say "I am God" is like one of my dreams or hiccups saying, "I am Lowell."

Human beings are interdependent. Nature and human-kind are interdependent. The quest for harmony is a categorical imperative as well a shrewd strategy for survival. "Oneness" is a poetic utterance based on this imperative. But within the Ping-Pong game to which each of us is confined, it is never a reality. I am I, and you are you. Here is my family, and there is yours. Here is my identity, and there is yours. Rules of right and wrong govern this here-and-now situation and always will. The poetic utterance "we are one" and the intuition that death is not final do not justify murder, violence, theft, rape, or even stealing this book. As long as we play the Ping-Pong game, the rules are final.

Individual human beings are conditioned and limited by their circumstances. At the same time, they are usually not as powerless as they believe. The ability of individuals to change circumstances, to transcend limitations through imagination, and to learn from others is utterly staggering.

Things happen. To find the meaning of what happens is a highly personal proposition. No one is greater than the myths governing his or her imagination. Our myths are as real as we are, and we are as real as our myths.

Some of the things that happen are weird, bizarre, exciting, frightening, and unexpected. The fact that something is exceptional does not mean that it is important—unless the one to whom it happens chooses to make it important.

There is magic. Sometimes it works, and sometimes it does not. Anyone who thinks that he or she can make it perform on demand is a fool.

Be aware of the "every-time-I-wash-the-car-it-rains" phe-nomenon. As Joel Achenbach observes, "Every time you wash the car it doesn't rain, it's just that when you wash the car and it does rain, it tends to stick in your mind."[5]

Things change. We change. We change because things change, and things change because we change.

Dr. Streiker's Metaphysical Laws of the Universe

So what lessons have I learned from my study of New Age and my personal deliberations on life in general? In the months spent conducting interviews; reviewing books, tapes, brochures, and periodicals; and musing about the personal, spiritual, ethical, and societal issues that came up for me, the following thoughts ran through my mind again and again.

Stop bitching. Complaints and gossip are more destructive than hurricanes. They also prevent the flow of power in one's life.

Don't make an ass of yourself. If something feels wrong, it probably is.

Love yourself.

Be lovable.

Avoid creeps.

Don't give your power away.

Remember that God has a sense of humor.

Beware of anecdotes. They prove everything and nothing. (Anecdotes are antidotes.)

Slow down. ''Too busy'' is always a lie. If there is no profit, you can't make it up with volume.

Simplify. If you don't really need it, get rid of it.

Complicate. A little sophistication never hurt anybody.

Keep your word, and let others know that you expect the same of them.

Create community. Invite into your life those persons who support what you cherish. Make your net work.

Say ''thank you''—especially to those through whom you have come to the light and to those who have loved you despite yourself.

Don't hurt anyone.

Resist frustrations, but accept limitations.

Remember your father on Mother's Day.

Be generous.

Work as though everything depends on you.

Enjoy life as though it all depends on God.

Love and serve. Nothing else matters.

For me, the key to life may be summarized in three assertions:

God is present in Jesus the Christ.

God demands perfection.

Striving cannot overcome imperfection; surrender and service can.

It has taken me eighteen words and a lifetime to say that—and I have probably used eighteen words too many.

Flying

I needed to test my power. So I walked from our apartment to a brick building on Ohio Street. The building's long stone staircase went, straight as an arrow, from the sidewalk to the second floor. I stood for a moment on the first stair, and I tried gliding to the sidewalk. Then I climbed another step and repeated the experiment—until I came to the fifth stair. I glided to the pavement, the shock to my feet and ankles sending a stinging sensation throughout my body. I was avoiding the intervening steps all right, but by jumping rather than flying.

Unknown to me until the final test, my friend Good Junior stood silent witness to my leaps. He joined me as I was rubbing the sting from my feet, his eyes and mouth competing to see which could open the most. ''Ma-dawn!'' he exclaimed. (''Ma-dawn,'' an invocation of Mary the Madonna, was Junior's all-purpose expletive.) He told me that he had never seen me jump more than two steps at once. (We used to have jumping contests on this particular staircase. Norton the Nemesis held the neighborhood record of four steps at a time.)

The next time we held a jumping contest, Junior told the gang what he had seen. No one believed him. They dared and taunted me and made fun of Junior until I responded. I managed two steps with no trouble. Trying from the third step took a lot of prompting from Junior, but I did it. At the fourth step, I froze, my arms swinging back and

185

forth as though I were about to take off, but my feet remaining fixed to the spot.

Mouthing insults ("Chicken!" "Sissy!"), the gang departed, leaving only Junior and me. He said nothing for a minute, just sat bouncing a tape-covered league ball on the cement. Then he looked up, peering at me, and then glanced at the fifth step. Without a word being spoken by either of us, I mounted the step, and with a single swing of my arms to propel me, I jumped gracefully to the pavement, feeling not the slightest sting. "Ma-dawn! Ma-dawn!" Junior exclaimed.

I still have many memories from those early days, the ten years (ages two to twelve) I spent at 635 North Springfield Avenue, on Chicago's near north side. Some of the memories are exhilarating and some frightening. And neither fifty years of life nor the wisdom of great books and learned professors, neither psychoanalysis nor hypnotherapy has enabled me to distinguish the events that really happened from those I only dreamed. Every now and then, when no one is looking, I want to climb a long, brass railed, marble staircase, push off, and glide to the bottom without touching a single stair as I descend.

Ma-dawn!

NOTES

Introduction

1. *This Hallowed Ground* (Garden City, N.Y.: Doubleday, 1956), p. 203.

1. What Is "New Age"?

1. Otto Friedrich, "New Age Harmonies." *Time* (Dec. 7, 1987): 62.
2. Russell Chandler, *Understanding the New Age* (Dallas: Word, 1988), p. 51.
3. Florence Graves, editorial, *The 1988 Guide to New Age Living* (Winter 1988): 3.
4. Brooks Alexander, "Moving Images: The New Age Movement and Christianity in the Media," *SCP Bulletin* (Fall 1988): 1.
5. *National & International Religion Report* (June 1988): 2.
6. Chris Kilham, Introduction to *In Search of the New Age* (Rochester, Vermont: Destiny Books, 1988), p. 1. Not to be confused with the remarkably complete and much more entertaining spoof of the New Age and other contemporary mail order religion (and anti-religion), the Reverend Ivan Stang's *High Weirdness by Mail* (New York: Fireside, 1988).
7. Ben Fong-Torres, "Journey Into the New Age." *San Francisco Chronicle* (April 28, 1988): B3-B4.
8. Ibid., p. B4.
9. Ibid., p. B5.
10. Ibid., p. B5.
11. Ben Fong-Torres, "A Cynic in the Midst of the Believers," *San Francisco Chronicle* (April 28, 1988): B5.
12. Jeremy P. Tarcher, "New Age as Perennial Philosophy." *New Realities* (May/June 1988): 27.
13. Ibid.
14. Ibid.
15. Ibid.
16. Ibid., p. 28.
17. Ibid.
18. Ted Peters, "Discerning the Spirits of the New Age." *The Christian Century* (Aug./Sept. 1988): 763.

187

19. Ibid., p. 766.
20. Ibid.
21. "A Personal Odyssey Thought the New Age." In *Not Necessarily the New Age*, ed. Robert Basil (Buffalo: Prometheus Books, 1988), p. 338.
22. Ibid., p. 339.
23. Ibid., p. 340.
24. Ibid., p. 341.
25. David Spangler, "Defining the New Age." *The New Age Catalogue* (New York: Doubleday, 1988), not paginated.
26. Ibid.
27. Interview by the author of Paul Zuromski, publisher/editor, and Carol Kramer, Managing Editor, at the offices of *Body, Mind & Spirit*, Providence, Rhode Island, June 27, 1988.
28. Terry Clifford, "The Master List." *New Age Journal* (Sept. 1976): 36.

2. New Age Forever

1. Robert S. Ellwood, Jr., *Alternative Altars: Unconventional Eastern Spirituality in America* (Chicago: University of Chicago Press, 1979), pp. 93-93.
 2. James Hutchinson Smylie, "New Thought." *The New Encyclopaedia Britannica* (Chicago: Encyclopaedia Britannica, Inc., 15th edition), 13:15.
 3. Ibid.
 4. J. Gordon Melton, *The Encyclopedia of American Religions* (Wilmington, N.C.: McGrath Publishing Company, 1978), volume 2.
 5. See Robert S. Ellwood, Jr., "Occult Movements in America." *Encyclopedia of the American Religious Experience* (New York: Charles Scribner's Sons, 1988), p. 717.
 6. Richard Blum, "Background Considerations." In Richard Blum et al., *Utopiates: The Use and the Users of LSD 25* (New York: Atherton, 1964), pp. 6-7 (italics added).
 7. R. E. L. Masters and Jean Houston, *The Varieties of Psychedelic Experience* (New York: Dell, 1967), p. 57.
 8. Ibid.
 9. Ellwood, *Alternative Altars*, p. vii.
10. Ibid., p. 7.
11. Joseph Campbell with Bill Moyers, *The Power of Myth* (New York: Doubleday, 1988), p. 158.
12. Ibid., p. 167.
13. Ellwood, *Alternative Altars*, p. 68.
14. Ibid., p. 7.
15. Ibid., p. 17.

3. New Age Comes to the Magazine Racks

1. Marilyn Ferguson, *The Aquarian Conspiracy: Personal and Social Transformation in the 1980s* (Los Angeles: J. P. Tarcher, 1980), p. 29.
 2. Graves, *The 1988 Guide to New Age Living*, p. 6.

3. Ibid., italics added.
4. Ibid.
5. Ibid., p. 12.
6. Ibid., p. 10.
7. Graves, *The 1988 Guide to New Age Living,* p. 3.

5. Stories

1. John Snow, *The Impossible Vocation: Ministry in the Mean Time* (Cambridge, Mass.: Cowley Publications, 1988), p. 138.
2. Ibid., p. 139.
3. Ibid., p. 146.
4. Ibid.
5. Ibid.
6. Ibid., p. 153.

7. The Witches of Salem

1. One of my Witch correspondents, Judy Harrow, has asked me to "please capitalize 'Witch' the same as you do Christian, and 'Goddess' the same as you do Jesus." She insists, "This is a matter of basic respect!" (letter of August 21, 1988).

   Harrow is the former president of the Covenant of the Goddess and is currently leader of the Proteus coven in uptown Manhattan. She has asked me to use her real name. Some of the Witches quoted in this chapter have requested that I substitute their respective "Craft names." As Beth A. Pollen, a Connecticut Witch, explains: "Some Witches feel comfortable in using their real names while others live in areas where they feel threatened if they reveal they are Witches to their friends, neighbors, work companions. Unfortunately, there are still many people who do not understand Witchcraft, and so fear it, and hate, fear and persecute its adherents" (letter of October 29, 1988).
2. "Witchcraft," *The New Encyclopaedia Britannica* (Chicago: Encyclopaedia Britannica, Inc., 15th edition, 1974), 19:899.
3. Margot Adler, *Drawing Down the Moon* (Boston: Beacon Press, 1986), p. 85.
4. Ibid.
5. One of my Witch correspondents adds: "Actually, the Horned God is usually seen as having two aspects—(1) the Green Man (e.g., Pan)—the young, lusty, and playful aspect of Nature. (2) The Hunter (e.g., Herne) representing fierceness, fear, and rough transformations. Both aspects are about wildness, passion, surprise, and freedom." Another explains more convincingly that the God has two aspects, the Horned God of the Hunt and the Green Man: The Horned God has horns because he is the Hunter and the Hunted. He is both that-which-kills and that-which-is killed. . . . The modern Christian image of the devil is a blasphemy against him. . . . The

Christian devil did not have horns before the Christians encountered worshipers of the Horned God! The Green Man is the divine force manifest in growing things, including, but not limited to, things planted and tended by humans.

6. EARTH-RITE, Mission San Jose, California, 415-651-9496 (Modem). Copyright © 1983 by Amber K., Our Lady of the Woods.

7. Men, as well as women, refer to themselves as Witches. The term *Warlock* is shunned, referring, say my Witch correspondents, to "oathbreakers" or Witches who turned in other Witches during the Burning Times in King James I's England.

8. See my discussion of God the Father in *Fathering—Old Game, News Rules* (Nashville: Abingdon Press, 1988), pp. 210-13.

9. Carol P. Christ, *Laughter of Aphrodite: Reflections on a Journey to the Goddess* (San Francisco: Harper & Row, Publishers, 1987), p. 36.

10. Ibid., p. 37.

11. Campbell and Moyers, *The Power of Myth*, p. 99.

12. Naomi R. Goldenberg, *Changing of the Gods: Feminism and the End of Traditional Religions* (Boston: Beacon Press, 1979), pp. 112-14.

13. In a telephone conversation with the author, July 14, 1988. Neither Dr. Rozman nor the University of the Trees is in any way affiliated with Wicca.

14. See Christ, *Laughter of Aphrodite*, p. 48.

15. See Goldenberg, *Changing of the Gods*, pp. 112-4.

16. See Diane Tennis, *Is God the Only Reliable Father?* (Philadelphia: The Westminster Press, 1985), pp. 27-28.

17. Ibid., p. 31.

8. New Age Religious Experience

1. "Watchbird" was a regular cartoon feature in a major women's magazine when I was a child. Its text went something like: "Here is a watchbird watching a thumb-sucker. Have you been a thumb-sucker this month?" The watchbird watching a malefactor would frown. The watchbird watching a nonmalefactor would smile.

2. Evelyn Underhill, *The Essentials of Mysticism* (New York: E. P. Dutton and Company, 1960), p. 18.

3. Ninian Smart, *Reasons and Faiths*, (London: Routledge & Kegan Paul, 1958), p. 71. See also Walter T. Stace, *The Teachings of the Mystics* (New York: New American Library, 1960).

4. See Sarvepalli Radhakrishnan and Charles Moore, eds., *A Sourcebook in Indian Philosophy* (Princeton: Princeton University Press, 1957), pp. 614-15.

5. Brhadaranyaka Upanishad, I.3.28.

6. David Baumgaurt, *Great Mystics* (New York: Columbia University Press, 1961), p. 7.

7. Alan W. Watts, *Nature, Man, and Woman* (New York: Pantheon Books, 1958), p. 160.

8. Rabindranath Tagore, *A Tagore Reader*, ed. Amiya Chakravarty (Boston: Beacon Press, 1961), pp. 333-34.

9. Stace, *The Teachings of the Mystics*, p. 17.
10. Ibid., p. 19.
11. Leo Schneidermann, "Psychological Notes on the Nature of Mystical Experience." *Journal for the Scientific Study of Religion* 6 (Spring 1967): 93.
12. I have counseled former members of a group in the Silicon Valley whose leader was a celebrated psychic counselor a few years ago and is now God's "prophet of the latter days." Prior to the Jonestown mass suicide, many of the defectors from the Peoples' Temple had become followers of California psychics or members of sectarian born-again groups.

9. UFOs, Health, and Death

1. David Weddle, "They're Here." *West San Jose Mercury News* (July 10, 1988): 17.
2. Ibid.
3. David Swift, "Epilogue: A Sociologist's Reaction." In Jacques Vallee, *Messengers of Deception* (Berkeley, Calif.: And/Or Press, 1979), pp. 226, 228-29.
4. Bernie S. Siegel, *Love, Medicine and Miracles: Lessons Learned About Self-Healing from a Surgeon's Experience* (Hagerstown, Maryland: Harper & Row, 1987), pp. 128-29.
5. Louise Hay, *Heal Your Body: The Mental Causes for Physical Illness and the Metaphysical Way to Overcome Them* (Santa Monica, Calif.: Hay House, 1982), p. 6.
6. Jason Serinus, ed., *Psychoimmunity and the Healing Process: A Holistic Approach to Immunity and AIDS* (Berkeley, Calif.: Celestial Arts, 1986). pp. 82-83.
7. Don Lattin, "New-Age Ministry Brings Self-Healing to the Battle with AIDS." *San Francisco Chronicle* (February 27, 1989): A9.
8. Spirit Speaks, *AIDS: From Fear to Hope: Channeled Teachings Offering Insight and Inspiration* (Los Angeles: Spirit Speaks, 1987), pp. 168-69. This book is a collection of channeled messages from Spirit Entities, which appeared in Spirit Speaks magazine.
9. Michael Lane and Jim Crotty, "Artist of the Monk . . . Stephen Frease." *Monk* 5 (1987): 59.
10. Michael Lane and Jim Crotty, "Artist of the Monk . . . Ly Le." *Monk* 4 (1987): 25.
11. Ibid., pp. 26-27.
12. Ibid., p. 27.
13. Beth Spring, "A Genuinely 'Good Death,' " *Christianity Today* (July 15, 1988): 28.
14. Jacques Vallee, *The Invisible College* (New York: E. P. Dutton, 1975), pp. 204-5.
15. Ibid., p. 206.
16. William Sadler, *The Physiology of Faith and Fear or the Mind in Health and Disease* (Chicago: A. C McClurg, 1925), p. vii.

10. New Age Meets the Gospel

1. Irenaeus, *Adversus Haereses*. In Henry Bettensen, ed. and trans., *The Early Christian Fathers* (London: Oxford University Press, 1956), p. 106.

2. Robert A. Raines, *The Ridge Leaf* (July 1988): 1.

3. Paul Boyer and Stephen Nissenbaum, *Salem Possessed: The Social Origins of Witchcraft* (Cambridge, Mass.: Harvard University Press, 1974), p. 30.

4. Campbell and Moyers, *The Power of Myth*, p. 220.

5. Joel Achenbach, "The Whys Have It," *San Jose Mercury News* (September 6, 1988): 1F.